Montana's Righteous Hangmen

MONTANA'S RIGHTEOUS HANGMEN

The Vigilantes in Action

By Lew. L. Callaway

Edited by Lew. L. Callaway, Jr.   Foreword by Merrill G. Burlingame

University of Oklahoma Press
Norman and London

Library of Congress Cataloging in Publication Data

Callaway, Llewellyn Link, 1868-1951.
  Montana's righteous hangmen.

  Includes index.
  1. Vigilance committees—Montana—Addresses, essays, lectures.
2. Frontier and pioneer life—Montana—Adresses, essays, lectures.
3. Montana—History—Addresses, essays, lectures. I. Callaway,
Llewellyn L. (Llewellyn Link), 1907–   . II. Title.
F731.C328   1981   364'.9786   81-40282
                    AACR2
ISBN: 0-8061-1728-1 (hardcover)
ISBN: 0-8061-2912-3 (paperback)

Portions of this volume were previously published in *Two True Tales of the
Wild West* (Oakland, Calif.: Maud Gonne Press, 1973).

3 4 5 6 7 8 9 10 11 12

To
ELLEN B. CALLAWAY
August 31, 1876–August 31, 1966

*Devoted wife of Llewellyn L. Callaway and
mother of five. A lively and beautiful lady
full of love, humor, and compassion.
She loved the Old West
of which she was a part.*

Contents

Contents

Illustrations

MAP

Foreword

By Merrill G. Burlingame

THE DISCOVERY OF gold in Montana is usually dated February 15, 1852, at Fort Owen, in the Bitterroot Valley, although the chief evidence is the brief note in John Owen's diary: "Gold Hunting. Found some."[1] Another discovery[2] was made in 1858 by James and Granville Stuart in the Deer Lodge Valley. This was widely publicized by them and led to the first big discovery at Bannack in 1862.

On May 26, 1863, the biggest and richest gold strike in the history of Montana, indeed, one of the largest in the world, was made along Alder Gulch, where Virginia City quickly became the center of activity. Over $100 million[3] has been taken from Alder Gulch, which is only fourteen miles long.

The discovery, made by the Bill Fairweather party of six men, attracted immediate attention in the Bannack gold camp

[1] Seymour Dunbar and Paul C. Phillips (Eds.), *The Journals and Letters of Major John Owen, 1851–1871*, 2 vols. (New York: Edward Eberstadt, 1927), 1:42.

[2] Granville Stuart, *Forty Years on the Frontier, as seen in the Journals and Reminiscences of Granville Stuart*, ed. Paul C. Phillips, 2 vols. (Glendale, N.Y.: Arthur H. Clark, 1957), 1:137–140.

[3] The official U.S. Mint price for gold in 1862 was $20.67.

Vigilante Country, 1863–64.

when the party sought to secure supplies with which to develop their new strike. Bannack was only seventy-five miles from Alder Gulch, and by June 6 a flood of gold seekers had reached the gulch, and Virginia City soon became the largest center of population in the interior Northwest.

A year later, May 26, 1864, Montana Territory was created. The continued rapid growth of the territory was assured by another fabulous gold discovery, that in Last Chance Gulch in July, 1864, where Helena sprang up immediately. Considerable political instability was created in the early years by fierce competition over which city would be the capital. It was moved from Bannack to Virginia City in 1865 and then to Helena in 1875.

The enormous migration of gold seekers who rushed into the Montana mining camps was stimulated to a great degree by the extensive discontent created over the entire United States by the civil war. The year 1863, which brought the tales of unlimited wealth to be obtained from the Montana mines, was also the decisive year of the war. In the first few days of July the fall of Vicksburg opened the Mississippi River and won the war for the Union in the West. At the same time the victory at Gettysburg stopped the advance of the Confederate Army in the East. During the war many people who had been uprooted by its destruction had fled to California, Colorado, and Nevada. The word of rich gold strikes brought them, along with many who were freed by the close of the war, to the northern mines in Montana and Idaho.

All kinds of people came. Only a few were miners. Many were farmers; but lawyers, doctors, editors, ministers, and businessmen came in large numbers, all hardworking and law-abiding. There were people from the North and from the South, Unionists and Confederates, still proudly bearing their battle scars. And the ne'er-do-wells also came. Draft dodgers, drifters, gamblers, saloonkeepers, and one of the largest collections of thieves and murderers ever to infest a community.

Some writers have said that Virginia City, Montana, and its small neighboring settlements, in the first years after gold discovery, became the most dangerous and bloodiest community ever seen in this country. Within two years after the discovery Virginia City had a population of ten thousand.

Gold's fierce lure brought murder and robbery into this land peopled by adventurers, mainly hardy males. Eventually the conditions of extreme danger brought into being an organization of law-abiding citizens known to history as the Vigilantes.

Judge Lew. L. Callaway in the stories of these brave men, *Montana's Righteous Hangmen*, opens a whole new vista on the personalities and the work of the Vigilantes of Montana. Long recognized as one of the most effective efforts to restore law and order in the American West, the Vigilantes have increasingly become the victims of rumor and innuendo. Judge Callaway, in recounting the insights which he and his father obtained through personal acquaintance with the leaders, explains the reasons for the great areas of silence and the absence of names from the early accounts of the movement. He has been almost alone in emphasizing the important point that the organization was not one of twenty or thirty secretive, vengeful, ambitious merchants but instead comprised as many as twenty-five hundred responsible men from every economic and social class in the several mining camps. He outlines the structure of this spontaneous association of outraged citizens and includes the "Regulations and Bye Laws" under which they operated.

Perhaps the outstanding contribution to this story of the Vigilantes is to reveal James Williams as a responsible, well-respected citizen of the community for many years. Williams has been acknowledged as the Executive Officer and guiding genius of the rough work of the Vigilante movement, but, by his own choice, he has been little known and has been particularly the target of suspicion and accusation. Through unusually close association Judge Callaway portrays Williams for the first time in both strength and weakness.

Joseph Slade has also been a shadowy, enigmatic personality. Judge Callaway says of him, "Probably no man in American history has been so misrepresented." This sketch presents a balanced view of his unusual characteristics of admirable courage and malicious bravado.

"The Story of George Ives" as told by Colonel Wilbur F. Sanders, the chief prosecutor of Ives, is a classic account of the work of the Miners' Court before the Vigilantes were organized. This trial is probably the most dramatic and famous criminal trial in the history of Montana.

During their lifetime both Colonel Sanders and Judge Callaway were favorite public speakers throughout the state. There was a widespread fear that they would not have time to record the firsthand impressions which they had of Montana's past. These accounts dispel that fear.

Editor's Preface

OVER THE YEARS the golden sands of Alder Gulch, Montana, have been worked and reworked by different mining methods but almost always with rich results.

Similarly many writers, professionals and amateurs, have found rich "diggings" in the highly adventurous, colorful, and bloody history of this same Alder Gulch and of Virginia City, which grew up on its banks. The principal stories in this book are about the dangerous years of 1863–64, which saw the emergence of the Vigilantes to overcome the criminal "road agents" and restore law and order in Alder Gulch and throughout the Territory of Montana.

Where have all the heroes gone? Well, a good many of them have been chronicled in these pages. The two foremost are the almost-unknown Captain James Williams, leader ("Executive Officer") of the Montana Vigilantes, and the justly famous Colonel Wilbur Fisk Sanders, chief prosecutor for the public in the trial of the notorious killer George Ives.

This part of Montana history is so thrilling and so dramatic that I have felt strongly that its story deserved retelling to as wide an audience as possible. That is why these oft-told tales of the Vigilantes and of Slade[1] are repeated here.

[1] The stories of the Vigilantes and of Captain Joseph A. Slade retold here first appeared in the *Weekly Madisonian* (Virginia City, Montana) and later

Lew. L. Callaway, my father, arrived in Virginia City, Montana, at the age of two with his father, Colonel James Edmund Callaway, and his mother, Mary Elizabeth Link Callaway. It was then March, 1871, and Colonel Callaway had come with his small family to take up his duties as secretary of the Territory of Montana. He had been appointed to this office, which was second in power to that of the governor, by President Ulysses S. Grant, who had been colonel and commanding officer of the Twenty-first Illinois Volunteer Regiment at the start of the Civil War. Colonel Callaway was serving in the same regiment as captain of Company D, the company that he had raised. He also served as Grant's adjutant while Grant, then a colonel, was in command of the regiment.

Colonel Callaway became partners with Captain James Williams in a ranch eighteen miles from Virginia City. As a young man his son, Lew. Callaway, lived and worked with Captain Williams and his sons and knew most of the leaders of the Vigilantes.

Tough times for the cattlemen of Montana and his father's herd, in particular, forced Lew. Callaway to drop out of school after the bad winter of 1886–87. He did not return to the Law School of the University of Michigan until 1889, and he graduated in the class of 1891.

In 1894 Lew. Callaway became county attorney of Madison County, Montana, and heard more firsthand stories of the activities of the Vigilantes from men who had taken an active part in their work. He served as mayor of Virginia City, Montana; judge of the Fifth Judicial District; and, from 1922 to 1935, chief justice of the Montana Supreme Court.

A ranch hand and cowboy himself, Judge Callaway loved

---

in a small paperback, *Two True Tales of the Old West* (Oakland, Calif.: Maud Gonne Press, 1973). To preserve the style of the era, they have been left as Judge Callaway originally wrote them.

Montana, enjoyed writing about those early days, and was an accurate chronicler of them. During his lifetime he was considered to be *the* authority on the Vigilantes and the famous Slade.

These stories of the early days of Montana demonstrate that indeed truth is often stranger than fiction. What Hollywood genius could dream up a more adventurous story than the restoration of law and order by the brave Vigilantes? Imagine the hardihood and dedication necessary to pursue criminals in below-zero weather on horseback in January, in Montana! How could a killer and cardsharp be elected sheriff in an honest election in Bannack in 1863? But Henry Plummer was both; and worse yet, he was also the secret head of a well-organized gang of murderers and thieves. Who can visualize a more chilling, colorful scene than the trial, conviction, and hanging of George Ives, murderer of young Nicholas Tbalt?

The "mother lode" for all writers about the Vigilantes has been, and still is, the classic, well-written *Vigilantes of Montana or Popular Justice in the Rocky Mountains*[2] by Professor Thomas J. Dimsdale, published in 1865. Professor Dimsdale was a fine journalist and an outstanding citizen of Virginia City, Montana. At a time when it took great courage to be an editor, he was the editor of the *Montana Post*, which first published his stories of the Vigilantes. He died at the untimely age of thirty-five, much mourned by the many who knew him.

It is always difficult to express adequate appreciation to all those who help make it possible for a book to reach the presses. The main credit for this volume, however, must go to Professor Emeritus Merrill G. Burlingame, who for thirty-eight years taught American and Montana history in Montana State University, Bozeman. In my opinion Professor Burlingame

[2] Thomas J. Dimsdale, *The Vigilantes of Montana* (Norman: University of Oklahoma Press, 1953).

knows more about the history of the Vigilantes than any other man living. With his help and that of Jim Vanderbeck of Virginia City, I have made an attempt to get the best possible pictures—some new—to illustrate the stories in this book. Also I am indebted to Professor Burlingame for the title of this book and the new map of Vigilante country. My lifelong Dartmouth friend and business associate at both *Time* and *Newsweek*, William Harris Scherman, gave liberally of his time and talent in the final stages of the manuscript. I am profoundly grateful to him for his help.

I have tried to give adequate credit through footnotes to the authors, books, and other sources quoted, and I am deeply grateful for these sources of information. William H. Bertsche, coauthor with Helen Fitzgerald Sanders of the excellent book *X. Beidler: Vigilante*, very kindly gave me permission to reprint the main part of "The Story of George Ives," written by Colonel Wilbur Fisk Sanders.

I also wish to express my appreciation to the staff of the Montana Historical Society for their indispensable help in aiding my research, in providing me with authentic pictures, and for giving me their constant interest, friendly help, and advice. Finally, my grateful appreciation to my editor Julia Grossman for her great skill and dedication in transforming some very good stories into what I hope our readers will think is a superior contribution to keeping alive the adventurous history of the Old West. My thanks too to my friend Edward A. Shaw for his friendly encouragement and constant interest in *Montana's Righteous Hangmen* and to all of his associates at the University of Oklahoma Press whose work meant so much to the completion of this book.

Lew. L. Callaway, Jr.

Napa, California

Montana's Righteous Hangmen

"Vigilante Ways," by O. C. Seltzer. Courtesy of the Thomas Gilcrease Institute of American History and Art, Tulsa.

CHAPTER ONE

Enter the Heroes and the Villains

Captain James Williams meets Joseph Alfred Slade. Stampede of gold seekers to Alder Gulch. Henry Plummer, secret leader of the outlaws elected sheriff, May 24, 1863. Robbery and murder rampant in Alder Gulch. Murder of Dillingham. His murderers acquitted.

AT THE TIME of his arrival in Alder Gulch, Captain James Williams was twenty-nine years old, a strongly built, slow moving man, 5-feet 10½ inches tall, weighing about 190 pounds. Upon slightly rounded shoulders a short neck carried a leonine head. He had deep-set blue eyes which were kindly and humorous, unless excited by deep emotion; then the eyes turned jet black, and in anger their menace was deadly. Take my word for it, the glance was terrifying! At such a time his voice was vibrant, of compelling timbre. Generally, however, he had excellent control of his faculties. In the years I knew him, while out of humor frequently, I saw him in deep anger only once.

Yet, according to all who knew him, this born leader, utterly without fear, was extremely reticent and self-effacing. Except at rare intervals he could not be induced to talk about himself, and he was especially silent concerning any occurrence dealing with his own prowess. He detested a braggart and seemed to think that if he told of an exploit reflecting

Captain James Williams, leader ("Executive Officer") of the Montana Vigilantes. Courtesy of the Montana Historical Society, Helena.

credit on himself, he would be suspected, if not accused, of boasting. Occasionally he would tell what happened in a natural and vivacious way and with an effort to minimize the importance of his own actions. It was his manner instead to emphasize what others did.

After the Vigilantes had completed their salutary but terrible tasks he made a studied effort to draw the veil of oblivion over their activities. He was not alone in this; many others of that sterling band also courted anonymity. His name does not appear in Dimsdale's famous narrative, at his own request. For this there appear to be two reasons. The more important, it seems to me, is that when the organization was created and engaged in its difficult but necessary work, everyone except the road agents and their sympathizers was applauding and cheering the Vigilantes on—but after the danger from the outlaws was over, the critics became vocal and the "anvil chorus" swelled. Indeed, some good people considered the Vigilantes themselves outlaws from the first, although condoning them somewhat because of the need which called the organization into being. Others feared the possession of so terrible a power in the hands of a few, unrestrained by law. Still others dreaded investigation. Most of the Vigilantes, and none more than Williams himself, detested their loathsome work, were sensitive to criticism, and wished to forget it.

Second, Dimsdale had asked Williams's financial support for his account. Williams was without vanity and preferred that the history not be written, and besides, he had not the means to comply with the request. The two men engaged in a mild argument during which Williams roughly ordered Dimsdale not to mention his name. Professor Dimsdale was of too large a calibre to permit pique to influence his pen, and so instead he frequently speaks in high praise of the "Executive Officer," "the leader," "the Captain."

There were others, while willing to aid in financing Dimsdale, who also asked that their names be withheld, some no doubt from fear of reprisal. Vows of vengeance coming from secret enemies were numerous enough to cause uneasiness—for none but the most unusual among men scorns threats of assassination. There are those, and there were some among the Vigilantes, notably Sanders and Williams, who seemed above the sense of fear.

About James Williams before he reached Montana: He was born on January 8, 1834, on a farm nine miles from Gettysburg, Pennsylvania. His father's parents were Welsh, his mother's Irish. They were Presbyterians, and extremely strict; perhaps that is why James left home when he was 19. It was rumored that he had been a sergeant in the army in Kansas in the border wars. He was what was called in those days a "free-state" man. After leaving Leavenworth, Kansas, in 1858, he came to Colorado, near Pikes Peak. It was all Kansas then, clear to the Rocky Mountains. During the next three years he was engaged in mining with his brother John. They were not too successful. Then he and John tried farming, first with good fortune, but then only to be wiped out by a cloudburst which swept away crops, horses, and everything else they had.

So in the spring of 1863, James sold out, intending to return to Pennsylvania, but the lure of the West was strong, and the report of rich discoveries of placer gold in Idaho drew his steps there. It was a hundred miles from his ranch to Denver and a long way from Denver to Bannack, center of the "Beaverhead mines" in Idaho, part of it through dangerous Indian country.

James Williams was about to enter upon new exciting and seemingly desperate adventures. A number of men, anxious to go to the new mines, joined with him; and when it came time to start upon the journey a respectable wagon train had assembled. Knowing the dangers ahead and having learned by experience the necessity of having a directing head, Williams was chosen captain, a title he was to bear through life. It was upon this expedition that he first encountered Captain Joseph A. Slade, that tremendous figure who, as overlord of the Julesburg division of the Overland Stage road, "was feared a great deal more, generally, than the Almighty, from Kearney, west," as Dimsdale wrote. Supporting testimony indicates that the two men met during the journey made by Williams and his party from Denver to Bannack. The story is that the train had not been upon its journey many days when it fell in with another headed by Slade. The parties camped together and the men became convivial; liquor flowed, and Slade fell a victim to his consuming vice.

When himself, probably there was no one upon the plains equal to Slade as an executive, no one superior to him in courage and sagacity, no one more gifted with the essential qualities of leadership. When sober he was a considerate and generous man, much the gentleman; when in liquor he was domineering, quarrelsome, and dangerous. With Slade under the influence of liquor, his men feared to go further into a country where the Indians were upon the warpath. They proposed, without Slade's knowledge, that the parties join for mutual protection. Williams and his men joined heartily in the suggestion; then someone said it would be wise to elect one captain for the two parties, and this was agreed upon. Williams's men preferred him, as did some of the Slade party; but others of Slade's men feared to excite his wrath. It was determined to elect a captain by popular vote.

When this came to Slade's attention, he became ugly and demonstrative. He said repeatedly that they could have all the elections they pleased, but he would be captain, tapping the scabbard enclosing his six-shooter. The danger was real; a man known to be a killer, reputed to have sent twenty-six men to

Bannack in the 1860s. Courtesy of Montana Historical Society.

the hereafter, was not to be trifled with. Williams, apprised of the situation and fully appreciating the tenseness of the occasion, acted with characteristic determination and courage. He sought out Slade, who was talking in a loud voice and gesticulating in a threatening manner.

Walking slowly to Slade, Williams looked him in the eye:

what Slade saw was enough to cause a complete change in his demeanor. Williams said, "Slade, I understand you say that no matter who is elected you will still be captain of this outfit. I want to say whoever is elected captain will be captain. Did you hear what I said?"

This menacing question, "Did you hear what I said?" was

often used by Williams when in deadly earnest. Slade, who knew a fighter when he saw one, smiled and said, "All right, Cap., that suits me."

Williams was elected almost unanimously. In after years he said, "I appointed Slade lieutenant, and I never had a man with me that I got along with better."

Fortunately the caravan got through the hostile Indian country without trouble, and the two parties separated at Soda Springs, as the Slade party was headed for Salt Lake. The Williams party arrived at Bannack about June 20, 1863. The camp was pretty much deserted, as most of the inhabitants had joined the stampede to Alder Gulch, a new discovery of reputed surpassing richness.[1] There Williams went about July 1st, locating at Nevada City, a small settlement near Virginia City. There were two thousand people in Alder Gulch at that time. All the ground along Alder Creek and upon the adjoining hillsides was already appropriated by prospectors who were living in tents, dugouts, or in the open air, too busily engaged in the pursuit of gold to build permanent structures. Some men were already erecting houses, and Williams entered into that activity. With his teams he soon got logs enough to build a number of cabins, 16 × 20—dirt roof and floor—which he sold for $200 each, yielding to him a good profit.

Before we go further, it will be well to name and locate the towns that were springing up in Alder Gulch. As the argonaut came from the Ruby Valley to the scene of the gold excitement, he first reached Junction, at the confluence of Granite and Alder creeks. A little over a mile up the the Alder he came to Adobetown, and a little less than a mile farther to Nevada ("Nevada City") situated on a small level plain along the east bank of the Alder. About a mile farther he reached

---

[1] For an account of a different kind of "gold rush" see Appendix A.

William H. Fairweather, leader of the discovery party that found gold in Alder Gulch. Courtesy of Montana Historical Society.

Central City, and from that point he went over the intervening ridge to Daylight Creek, dropping rapidly into the roaring camp named Virginia City, situated at the confluence of Daylight and Alder creeks. At that time there was no road along Alder Creek from Central City to Virginia City. Above Virginia City the traveler followed the Alder Canyon, passing settlements at the mouths of Hungry Hollow and Butcher Gulch and the little towns of Pine Grove and Highland, before reaching Summit City, a considerable mining camp at what was deemed the head of Alder Gulch.

Men were pouring into Alder Gulch by the hundreds, bringing little with them, and the necessities of life were low in the increasingly great camp. It was four hundred miles to Salt Lake, and Fort Benton was not yet looked to as a source of supply; indeed, no steamboat arrived at Benton in 1863. Supplies were to be had at Elk City in Idaho territory, where extensive placer mining was in progress; and, until the Salt Lake Road was well established, considerable quantities of freight were transported by pack animals from that source.

The trail from Virginia City to Elk City was long. It ran down Alder Gulch and the Ruby Valley to the present Twin Bridges and crossed the Beaverhead and Big Hole rivers. It then took the Indian trail over the ridge, passing over the ground where the mining camp of Rochester was to be. It crossed Camp Creek and Moose Creek and followed up Divide Creek to the summit of the Rocky Mountain. It then descended to Silver Bow Creek and ran over the ridge, the "Hump," to meet the continuation of Silver Bow Creek, called successively Deer Lodge River, Hellgate River, and Missoula. It followed this river to its confluence with the Bitterroot. (This is the route which the Lewis and Clark expedition would have taken had it been led by a guide familiar with the country, but of

Henry Edgar, member of the Fairweather Party that discovered the rich gold of Alder Gulch. Courtesy of the Thompson-Hickman Historical Museum, Virginia City, Montana.

course they did not have any such guide.) The route then went up the Bitterroot to Fort Owen, over the Bitterroot range by the southern Nez Perce trail, and over the Bitterroot Mountains to Elk City on the upper reaches of the south fork of the Clearwater.

For some weeks Williams engaged in the slow and arduous business of transporting freight by pack horses from Elk City to the Alder Gulch settlement. The tariff was $1 per pound, but even at that price there was little profit to be gained. Freighting between Virginia City and Salt Lake City by team presented a different aspect, however. Williams and John Martin formed a partnership to carry on a feed stable in Nevada City, with freighting in connection. A four-mule freight-team was kept upon the road between Salt Lake and Virginia City, with gratifying results. In the meantime Captain Williams and his brother John located a ranch on Williams Creek (named for them), a tributary of the Ruby River, four or five miles south of Nevada, upon which they maintained a considerable number of work and saddle horses. The ranch was run in conjunction with the stable business in Nevada.

The possession of this stable, fifty or sixty head of saddle horses, and twenty-five saddles and bridles became an important factor in the life of Alder Gulch, to say nothing of a farther-reaching effect, very soon.

One Henry Plummer was elected sheriff of Bannack district on May 24, 1863, at a miners' meeting presided over by Walter Booth Dance, president of the district, with D. H. Dillingham acting as secretary. That the election was a fair one can hardly be doubted. It was held to elect a judge, sheriff, and a coroner (certainly a coroner was needed!) for the district. B. B. Burchette and J. M. Castner, respectively elected judge and coroner, were men of probity. The presiding officer, "Judge" Dance, was a man of undoubted integrity; indeed, he was for many years a distinguished citizen and servant of Montana Territory. (Of Dillingham, the clerk, more later.)

The election of Plummer is one of the strangest episodes in American history. Over five hundred votes were cast and Plummer received a large majority. A respectable minority distrusted the man and supported Jefferson Durley. It is true that Plummer's long record of betrayal and murder was unknown to the people of Bannack, unless to a few of his former associates; and they wisely kept still. Probably Plummer arrived in Bannack as early as November, 1862. In January, 1863, he shot to death Jack Cleveland, the one man in the camp who knew his entire bloody history; but this altercation was deemed merely a fight between gamblers. The fact that Plummer was a professional gambler did not seem to impress the majority unfavorably. It was true also that he had had trouble with Crawford, his predecessor as sheriff. Crawford had shot Plummer through the right arm when Plummer was not looking and had seriously crippled "the quickest man on trigger in the mountains." Plummer was obliged to learn to shoot with the left hand, becoming unusually proficient in a short time.

Plummer had the appearance and address of a gentleman, an attractive personality—especially ingratiating with women—and a manner which inspired confidence in most men. He was, in fact, a cold-blooded, calculating villain, secretive to the last degree, possessed of great organizing and executive ability. He seems to have been something of a politician.

The day before the election he purchased lot No. 10 on Second Cross Street in Bannack with the announced purpose of building a residence there; he intended to be married in a few days to a lady at Sun River crossing. Elected, he announced the appointment of his deputies: D. H. Dillingham, chief deputy; Buck Stinson, Ned Ray, and Jack Gallagher, deputies.

Who was Dillingham, and what were his relations with Plummer? Various answers have been given. At the time of his appointment as chief deputy he was highly regarded by all; after his death some thought him an ordinary road agent. Others said he was a detective who wormed his way into Plummer's confidence for the express purpose of running to earth Plummer's associates, Charley Forbes, Buck Stinson and Haze Lyons, fugitives from justice. Others thought, and the truth seems to be, that Dillingham was an honest man whom Plummer selected to give his office at least a semblance of respectability, for Stinson, Ray, and Gallagher were "roughs," criminals; and Plummer knew what they were. Indeed, it is likely his road-agent band had already been organized.

Having named his office force, with the honorable Dillingham in charge, Plummer set out to marry his sweetheart, the lovely Electa Bryan, sister of the wife of J. A. Vail, manager of the government farm at the crossing of the Sun River on the Mullan Road. Poor, little Electa Bryan, what a disillusionment awaited her!

Plummer reached Sun River on June 2nd. Thus news of the discovery at Alder Gulch had not reached Bannack when he left on his love quest, and he did not return to his seat of power until Virginia City was in the first throes of its turbulent early life, for the wedding did not take place until June 20th.

Mr. and Mrs. Plummer, traveling by government ambulance—borrowed at Sun River—at best probably did not make over forty miles a day, and the way was long. As soon as the sheriff reached Bannack, he dispatched Dillingham and Stinson to Virginia City, thus extending his sway as sheriff a distance of 70 miles from Bannack. When Plummer organized his road-agent band cannot be ascertained; but, as suggested above, it was probably before he was elected sheriff. Granville Stuart, writing of conditions at Bannack in April, 1863, said:

The rich "diggings" of Grasshopper Creek attracked many undesirable characters and I believe there were more desperadoes and lawless characters in Bannack the winter of 1862–63 than ever infested any other mining camp of its size. Murders, robberies, and shooting scrapes were of frequent occurrence.

These were dark days in Bannack; there was no safety for life or property only so far as each individual could, with his trusty rifle, protect his own. The respectable citizens far outnumbered the desperadoes, but having come from all corners of the earth, they were unacquainted and did not know whom to trust. On the other hand the "Roughs" were organized and under the leadership of that accomplished villain, Henry Plummer. At times it would seem that they had the upper hand and would run affairs to suit themselves. The law abiding citizens were beginning to get better acquainted and although the few attempts made to administer justice had failed they believed that the time would come and that at no distant day, when the community would rid themselves of this undesirable element.

When Alder Gulch began to pour out with lavish hand her golden treasures, robbery and murder became the order of the day. Terror overspread the mining camps of Grasshopper and Alder and the tributary country; the roads were ways of peril.

Colonel Sanders wrote:

Late in the summer of 1863 it began to dawn upon the Virginia City citizens that these highway robbers were plying their vocation with great industry, but as they dominated the executive offices of the volunteer tribunals the mouths of the suspicious were sealed. With increasing certainty and ever-widening scope, this open secret, at first a suspicion, grew into an absolute certainty, told in whispers; and strangers in the country who had gained each other's confidence, began to consult as to the protection of their enterprises and themselves, and even dared to speak confidentially the names of the guilty parties.

Virginia City, Montana Territory, 1866. Looking east up Wallace Street. Courtesy of Montana Historical Society.

How many men were members of the road-agent band it is impossible to say. The inner circle may easily have numbered fifty, a hundred more may have been allied to the central organization more or less closely, and Plummer seems to have had the confidence of all the roughs. The vast majority of the inhabitants were law-abiding people, who had come from the best middle-class homes in the country, and the middle class is ever the backbone of a nation. Nearly all had attended the schools in their home states, many were highly educated. They believed in a government by law and had no confidence in a government unrestrained by law. They proposed to have law and order, but there were no courts, save the poor device of a "miners' court," west of Yankton, north of Salt Lake, east of Walla Walla. Such people could not long endure the perils which beset them, could not live under constant terror. The mass required leadership, but it required a crisis to produce the leaders.

The situation was accentuated by the murder of Dillingham, chief deputy. He must have learned early the methods used by the road agents. Two stage coaches were running daily between Virginia City, via Bannack, to Salt Lake—one by A. J. Oliver & Co. and the other by Peabody & Caldwell—conveying passengers and express, consisting chiefly of gold dust. Of course, many of the passengers carried the precious dust. Plummer and his deputies, by reason of their official positions, knew when important shipments were being made. Cabalistic marks were made upon coaches indicating to the road agents whether robbery was to be done, and this practice was soon extended to ordinary vehicles; robbery and murder were common. Being in Bannack early in September, Dillingham learned that G. W. Stapleton, a man named Dodge, and another, who were going to Virginia City by coach, were to be robbed on the way by Forbes, Stinson, and Lyons. Dillingham warned

Dodge, who foolishly told Forbes what he had learned. This sealed Dillingham's fate.

Fearing to commit the robbery, Stinson, Lyons, and Forbes abandoned that project but determined to kill Dillingham; and the opportunity soon came. Dillingham was in Virginia attending a miners' court presided over by Dr. Steele, afterwards mayor of Helena and a prominent citizen of this state. Calling their victim away from the brush "wickiup" (Bannack Indian for lodge or teepee), in which the court was being held, Forbes, Stinson, and Lyons shot him to death. The three were arrested and kept under guard.

Williams with others stood guard over them the night preceding their trial. At the trial three judges presided, sitting in a wagon while all the people presided as jurors. Stinson and Lyons were tried first, promptly found guilty, and sentenced to hang. John X. Beidler, soon to rise to fame as a Vigilante and upholder of the law, with the assistance of one Dick Sapp, promptly erected a scaffold for the execution and dug graves for the condemned. Meanwhile the trial of Forbes proceeded. He was fraudulently acquitted. When it came time to hang Stinson and Lyons, friends of theirs manipulated so that another vote was taken, then another, and still another. The upshot was that they were released also.

The decent people of the community felt outraged beyond measure. Their feelings were not mollified when Forbes and Lyons went to the newly dug graves and made vulgar sport there. In so doing Lyons fairly kicked Fate in the face; for within four months he found a final resting place in one of those graves. Forbes died at the hands of his fellow outlaws even before that.

CHAPTER TWO

The Notorious Killer George Ives Murders Young Nicholas Tbalt

Tbalt's body miraculously found. Captain James Williams and a posse capture Ives. Trial and hanging of George Ives. Heroic role of Colonel Wilbur Fisk Sanders as chief prosecutor of Ives.

AFTER THE acquittal of Dillingham's murderers, matters went rapidly to the extreme in Alder Gulch. Scarcely a day passed without a serious affray of some sort. Common brawling was so frequent as to cause little excitement except among the immediate participants, and not much comment by anybody. Among the road agents George Ives was conspicuous. He was a tall young man, extremely affable, and called handsome, but with a sinister glance which he cultivated with some pride. He was a dangerous, cool-headed, fearless villain whom everybody dreaded, and none more than his associates. A long list of crimes, including robbery and murder, was credited to him.

A short time before the fateful December of 1863 he had waylaid and killed a young man near the Cold Spring Ranch on the public road, in plain sight of two ranch houses and two or three teams traveling the road, because the man had threatened to give information concerning the road agent. Dimsdale relates that Ives fired first at his victim with a shotgun loaded

22

with buckshot, but as the buckshot did not penetrate suffi-
ciently to kill, he drew a revolver and, talking to the man all
the while, shot him dead. He then took his victim's horse and
disappeared into the hills. No action was taken to punish the
murderer. But the murder of Nicholas Tbalt, a mere boy, by
Ives in the forepart of December, 1863, brought matters to a
head. Tbalt had sold to Clark and Burtschy, his employers, a
span of mules for which they had paid him $200 in gold. Tbalt
went to Dempsey's ranch, where the mules were on pasture,
with the intention of delivering them to Clark & Burtschy
at Summit, the upper camp in the Alder Gulch settlement.
Tbalt passed the night at Dempsey's, which without Dempsey's fault was a road-agent rendezvous, and it is likely the boy
disclosed the fact that he had gold upon his person. Setting
out the next morning with the mules, he was overtaken and
killed by Ives, who took the gold from his person and the work
mules to a ranch on the Big Hole River, occupied by a man
named Bourbon. When Tbalt did not return, Clark and Burtschy concluded that the boy had run away with mules and
money. Tbalt was not found for ten days, when by accident, a
seeming miracle, his body was revealed: "It was the finger of
God that indicated the scene of the assassination," says Dimsdale. Indeed it does appear that the hand of Providence inter-
posed to bring to justice the murderer. William Palmer, on his
way to Alder Gulch, was crossing the Ruby Valley, walking
ahead of his team, shotgun upon his shoulder. A grouse rose,
Palmer fired, and the bird fell through the willows upon the
frozen body of Nicholas Tbalt. Quoting Dimsdale, the graphic, again: "The marks of a small lariat were on the dead man's
wrists and neck. He had been dragged through the brush while
living, after being shot, and when found lay on his face, his
right arm bent across his chest and his left hand grasping the
willows above him."

The same authority relates that Palmer asked two of Plummer's men, Long John and Hilderman, who were camped about a quarter of a mile distant, to assist him in putting the corpse in a wagon that it might be taken to town and identified, and they said, "No. That's nothing. They kill people in Virginia everyday, and there's nothing said about it. We want to have nothing to do with it."

Nevertheless Palmer took the body to Nevada City for identification. After they had arrived there, many people viewed the body and talked of the circumstances under which it was found. The strange disappearance of Nicholas Tbalt was discussed; some said, "this may be Tbalt." "I'll find out if it's Tbalt," said William Heron, who saddled his horse and rode the nine miles to Summit. Returning with Albert B. Hamilton, Elkanah Morse, and George Burtschy, the identity of the victim was established; but who was the murderer?

"One of that damned band of cutthroats, and he's right down there with those fellows who wouldn't help Palmer," someone explained.

At the height of the excitement William Clark, generally known as "Old Man" Clark, went to Williams and suggested the organization of a vigilante committee. He said, "This thing has been running on long enough and has got to be stopped."

He was for immediate action and seems to have been the first starter of the movement. Prior to this a good deal of talk along this line had been made by different people, but it had no effect except to cultivate public sentiment that way. Williams told Clark he had 50 or 60 head of saddle horses and 25 or 30 saddles and bridles which could be used to equip a party for the arrest of the killer. The response was immediate; the party organized during the late afternoon, some going to the Williams ranch for horses. Williams furnished horses, saddles, and bridles to those who asked for them. William Clark was "rarin' to go." Equally determined were Elk Morse, Albert B. Hamilton, George Burtschy, X. Beidler, J. S. Daddow, Charles Brown, Thomas Baume, William Palmer, and others whose names are not ascertainable with certainty now, about 12 in all. Elk Morse was elected captain, and he justified the confidence reposed; he was cautious, cool, and brave.

Williams had not intended to go (he was too busy outfitting the party), but someone said, "Come on, Cap, we can't go without you," and the others to a man urged him to go. His adventurous spirit could not resist. The party got away about ten o'clock, upon a cold winter night.

Shortly after midnight, after a rapid ride they reached a ranch house where they stopped to warm. Within, were five or six men playing cards, and one of them, Jack Reynolds by name, recognized Hamilton. Calling Hamilton aside, Reynolds asked where the party was going and begged to be allowed to go along. Hamilton told his companions he knew Reynolds to be a reliable man, a good shot, and quick with a gun. Fortunately, it was decided to permit Reynolds to join the party, for as it turned out he rode the best horse in the posse.

It was known that the road agents, including Long John, who was suspected of the murder because of his actions at the time Tbalt's body was found, were camped on Wisconsin Creek some six or seven miles below Dempsey's. When within a mile of the road-agent camp, the party dismounted to wait until daylight. The orders were to maintain quiet. For two seemingly endless hours they waited for daylight, the silence of the winter night being broken only by the muffled tones of the men tramping in the snow to keep from freezing and the snuffling of the horses. At the first sign of day they mounted and rode rapidly toward their quarry. As they came near the wickiup, a dog barked, and the posse, following out a previous order of Captain Morse, surrounded the camp with guns pointing toward it. Williams's position was immediately in front of the entrance of the wickiup. Here his natural instinct for leadership asserted itself. Seeing a number of men who were sleeping on the ground in front of the wickiup "stirring as if coming to life," he leaped from his horse, leveled his short double-barreled shotgun upon them, and said, "The first man that moves gets a quart of buckshot!"

All kept still in their beds. Going to the wickiup and throwing back the flap, he ordered, "Hands up!" and said, "Is Long John here?"

"Yes. What do you want?"

"You to come along and ask no questions."

Williams, Morse, and two others then took Long John some distance away from the others and charged him with the murder. They did not take him to the scene of Tbalt's murder as reported by Dimsdale, who says they went on foot to that place; it was at least six miles distant from the road agent camp. John vigorously denied any participation in the robbery and murder of Tbalt. Being shown J. X. Beidler's saddle mule which Tbalt had ridden to get the mules, and reproached for his actions when the body was discovered, John broke down; he said he did not do it but that one of the men who did do it was at the wickiup, George Ives.

Williams seems to have continued the actual leadership from this time on. Leaving the prisoner in the hands of his companions, Williams went alone to the wickiup. Throwing back the flap which served as a door, Williams stepped inside and said, after the preliminary warning of hands up, "George Ives, I want you."

"What for?"

"To go to Virginia City."

"All right," Ives replied, "I guess I'll have to go."

Two members of the posse, seeing "Old Tex" with the road agents and knowing him to be a first-class villain, arrested him also. Having Ives, Long John, and Old Tex in custody, the members of the posse became careless. Being hungry as well as cold, they disposed themselves about the camp fire, eating, and drinking coffee. Their arms were laid about carelessly. In their midst were Alex Carter, Whiskey Bill, Bob Zackary, and Johnny Cooper, redhanded cutthroats, fully armed, desperate, and unrestrained. To be sure, all, following the cue of Ives, were affable in the extreme. Apparently they treated the arrest as a joke. Williams was not misled by these actions; his border war experiences stood him well in hand. He commanded in a voice charged with meaning, "You fellows hang on to your guns."

Dimsdale says, "In after expeditions he had no need to re-peat the command."

This identifies Williams as the actual leader at the time, for he was the only one of the entire posse who afterwards had charge of an expedition. The party then took its way home-ward, picking up Hilderman at Dempsey's. At Ives's request he was permitted to ride his own horse; the reason for the request soon developed. The road between the Cold Spring Ranch and Daley's (the Robbers' Roost) on Ramshorn Creek was good. Soon impromptu horse races were being run, Ives keeping his horse well to the front. As they neared Daley's, a race was run from which Ives's horse emerged a winner by many lengths, and he kept right on. The posse awoke to the fact that their prisoner was escaping. Reynolds, Hamilton's friend, put spurs to his horse, pressing Ives so hard that he was unable to make a transfer to a fleet horse, which was standing saddled and bridled at the Robbers' Roost for his use. Ives was in the lead with Reynolds next, then Burtschy, and then the

"Robbers Roost near Virginia City, Montana," by O. C. Seltzer. Courtesy of Gilcrease Institute.

posse, well strung out along the road but keeping the other prisoners well in hand. Ives started up Biven's Gulch but was headed off. He then made for Alder Gulch, keeping his horse at top speed. The horse fell, exhausted, near the rocky butte about a half mile below Alder Canyon. Ives ran down a ravine and into the willows, Reynolds close behind him. Burtschy not far behind. Ives was well concealed in the willows, but after hunting closely for a time, Burtschy spied him and he was taken into custody again. Thereafter he rode with his hands tied behind him and his feet tied one to the other beneath the horse's belly. The halter was suggestive of the hanging to come.

The party got into Nevada well toward evening and paused in front of Lott Brothers' store to report the capture. John Lott appeared and observed the prisoners.

"What are you going to do with them?" he asked.

"Take them to Virginia City."

"No," Lott said, "if they are tried there, we'll have another Dillingham mess. Let's try them here in Nevada City."

Mortimer H. Lott, who presently appeared, supported his brother's argument with vigor. He got upon a dry goods box and addressed the crowd, by now several hundred, predicting what would happen in all probability if Ives were taken to Virginia City, and he moved that the prisoners be tried in Nevada City. The motion carried, and Williams said, "We will hold them here in Nevada."

That settled it. Ives, Hilderman, and Long John were heavily chained—a log chain being used—and guarded in a house which stood within the enclosure containing the Fenner residence.

I will not here attempt a detailed description of the great trial that followed. That has been given adequately by Colonel Sanders, except that he minimized his own part in it. [See Appendix B.]

Certainly the setting was picturesque. The trial was held in the main street of Nevada City, consuming a portion of December 19th and all of the 20th and the 21st, heat being supplied by fires built in the open. The court consisted of Judge Byam and Associate Judge Wilson, a jury of 24 men, W. Y. Pemberton and W. H. Patten acting as clerks. As is known to all, Colonel Sanders was chief counsel for the people. With him was associated Major Charles S. Bagg, who prosecuted with great ability and zeal; but Bagg was cast in the shadow by the masterly talents of the brilliant and fearless Sanders. Ives was represented by four counsel, who labored earnestly for his acquittal.

During the trial order was preserved by the miners' sheriffs, Robert Hereford of the Nevada District and Adriel B. Davis of the Junction District; but at all times, around judges, jury, prisoner, lawyers, clerks, and sheriffs, stood a circle of 100 armed men under the command of James Williams. Surrounding the guards, there was another circle composed of hundreds, mostly miners, who took a considerable part in the trial; one frequently would arise to his feet and present his ideas as to the manner in which the proceeding should be conducted. Arguments were proffered by individuals in the crowd respecting the reception of testimony. It is perhaps unnecessary to say that objections by counsel for the defense respecting the admission of testimony were generally overruled. Technical objections found no favor before that tribunal! The evidence concluded, eloquent and forceful arguments were presented, first by Major Bagg for the people, then by counsel for the prisoner. Sanders closed for the people.

Shortly after the conclusion of Sanders's masterful closing

"Recapture of George Ives, by the Vigilantes, Madison County, Montana, December 20, 1863," by O. C. Seltzer. Courtesy of Gilcrease Institute.

speech, the jury returned a verdict of guilty; 23 of the 24 who signed the verdict, one[1], for prudential reasons it is supposed, did not sign. It was now about six o'clock in the evening. Upon the rendition of the verdict, Sanders, having in mind the fiasco which resulted in the escape of Dillingham's murderers, arose and moved that whereas George Ives had been found guilty of murder "he is forthwith [to be] hanged by the neck until he is dead."

This motion was addressed to the multitude, which favored it by a great majority, although perhaps more than a hundred shouted "No!" Ives now appreciated the seriousness of his predicament; before, he had assumed an apparent air of nonchalance, perhaps thinking the powerful and resourceful Plummer would effect his rescue. Rising from his seat upon the ground near the log fire, the condemned man climbed upon the wagon and addressed Sanders, who he perceived then dominated the assemblage, and was the director of his fate. Without any show of trepidation he requested a postponement of the execution until the morrow in order that he might make his will and write to his mother and sisters. While Sanders was reflecting upon the manner of speech which he would choose in denying the request, the irrepressible X. Beidler, seated with his shotgun upon the low dirt roof of a nearby building, sang out, "Sanders, ask him how much time he gave the Dutchman [Tbalt]!"

This brought a laugh from the crowd, and Sanders, relieved, told Ives he should have thought of the matter sooner and to get down; he might have time to write a letter before the sheriffs returned. Those officers, in the meantime, had been preparing a place for the execution. They chose a nearby building which was in the process of erection, the log walls

[1] According to Colonel Sanders the one man who did not sign was Henry Spivay.

Colonel Wilbur Fisk Sanders, chief prosecutor for the public in the trial of the murderer George Ives. Courtesy of Montana Historical Society.

having reached the intended height, ready for the roof. A scaffold was made by placing a beam 30 feet or more in length on the top log of the easterly side of the building, the large end resting on the ground under the bottom log on the west side. A rope in which Davis had tied a hangman's knot was fastened to the small end of the log, and there it dangled—a weird spectacle in the ghastly firelight—over a box upon which the prisoner was to stand. The spot was lighted by a great fire, built as if to accentuate the terror of the scene.

It was eight o'clock, and Williams had thrown his armed guard about the place of execution. The most dangerous moment in the entire transaction had arrived. Threats were made that no man should live to adjust the noose. Ives's friends, the road agents, the thieves, the lawless, stood all about fully armed. Yet Davis got upon the box as coolly as if about to do an ordinary act. The crowd stirred ominously—some present always asserted that the air was disturbed by the cocking of many six-shooters—and then came the sharp command from Williams, "Men! 'Bout face! Prepare to shoot!"

A hundred men in the crowd turned to run away.

The rope was found too long to allow a drop—Ives's feet would touch the ground. So Davis "shinned up" the log and shortened the rope. When Ives mounted the box the rope still seemed too long, whereupon Bennett, a partner of W. B. Carter, late well-known citizen of Dillon, volunteered to shorten it still more. Before doing so he told Carter what disposition to make of his effects in case he did not come down alive. The rope now being short enough, Davis adjusted the noose. Williams said, "Men, do your duty."

The box was jerked from under Ives and the deed was done.

The effect was tremendous. Outlawry in Montana foresaw its finish. Honest men heaved a sigh of relief. Everybody but the road agents felt safer.

CHAPTER THREE

Organization of the Vigilance Committee

The names and titles of the officers of the Vigilance Committee. The oath of the Vigilantes. "Regulations and Bye Laws."

THE ORGANIZATION of the Vigilance Committee followed. The exact details are obscure, and have always been the subject of trifling controversies.

As may be supposed, during a period when no man's life was safe, those who were not in league with or under the protection of the outlaws were discussing some means of relief. Outstanding citizens—Langford, Sanders, and others at Bannack, and Paris S. Pfouts, the Lotts, and others in Alder Gulch— had said more or less openly that conditions were crying for a Vigilance Committee. There was an immediate historical background for an organization of that character. Pfouts was a resident of San Francisco when the Vigilantes under William T. Coleman were engaged in their salutary work, and he had great admiration for that extraordinary man, Coleman. Pfouts, Williams, the Lotts, Davis, and others had recently come from Denver, where a Vigilance Committee, patterned after the one in San Francisco, had been cleaning up the town.

As has been said, William Clark had suggested to Williams

"The Vigilante's Oath—Organization Meeting, December 20, 1863," by O. C. Seltzer. Courtesy of Gilcrease Institute.

the necessity of such a committee before the party set out to capture the slayer of Tbalt. It is not unusual for men acting independently but dominated by the same thought to do pretty much the same thing, even to the extent of expressing themselves in almost identical language, at the same time. So it is not a cause for doubt that men in Virginia City and Nevada City, without the knowledge of each other, were driven to the same end in the same way. Dimsdale, whose information was obtained at first hand, has this to say:

> Two sister towns—Virginia and Nevada—claimed the honor of taking the first steps towards the formation of a Vigilance Committee. The truth is, that five men in Virginia and one in Nevada commenced simultaneously to take the initiative in the matter. Two days had not elapsed before their efforts were united, and when once a beginning had been made the ramifications of the league of safety and order extended in a week or two all over the Territory . . .
>
> The reasons why the organization was so generally approved, and so numerously and powerfully supported, were such as appealed to the sympathies of all men who had anything to lose, or who thought their lives safer under the domain of a body which, upon the whole, it must be admitted, has from the first acted with a wisdom, a justice, and a vigor never surpassed on this continent, and rarely, if ever equalled.

In Virginia City the leaders were Paris S. Pfouts and Wilbur F. Sanders. Mr. Pfouts writes that during the Ives trial "five gentlemen held a secret meeting in Virginia City and determined upon the formation of a Vigilante Committee. These five men were Nick Wall of St. Louis, Col. Wilbur F. Sanders, Maj. Alvin V. Brookie, John Nye and myself. We agreed to hold another meeting the following night, and each one of us was to bring such other gentlemen as were willing to unite

Paris S. Pfouts, president, or chief, of the Vigilantes. Courtesy of Montana Historical Society.

with us in the cause, but the utmost caution was to be observed in inviting none but those known to be trustworthy."

The one man in Nevada City referred to by Dimsdale must
have been John S. Lott. It is not likely that Williams was the
Nevada man. He was busy holding his volunteers together,
guarding Ives, preserving order, and watching against attempts on the part of the road agents to effect a rescue of the
prisoner. Again, Lott was inclined to take the initiative and
Williams was not; Williams's forte was as an executive. If
the writer felt constrained to name the exact date upon which
the men of Virginia City and Nevada City actually formed the
Vigilance Committee, he would be confronted with an insolu-
ble task upon the basis of present knowledge. Whether the
meeting was on the day after the demise of Ives or three days
later, and to the historical analyst there is much evidence each
way, is not of much importance. In either event, the conditions considered, the actors proceeded with great celerity.

Adriel B. Davis gives this account:

In about three days after the hanging of Ives the original Vigilante
Committee, that is, the first twelve, were sworn in as Vigilantes in
Fox's blue house, which formerly stood where the Masonic Temple is
now on Wallace Street in Virginia City. . . . The meeting was called
by Paris Pfouts and Sanders; when we got there it was suggested that
we organize a Vigilante Committee for self-protection. Among those
present were Wilbur F. Sanders, Paris S. Pfouts, James Williams,
J. M. Fox, A. B. Davis, John S. Lott, Elkanah Morse, and a young
man who clerked in McClurg's store, whose name I have forgotten
and can't get, but he was from California and was the one who
administered the oath to us.

It is likely that the memory of the usually reliable Davis
failed him here; that would not be strange, for unless a man
who is contemporaneous with an event puts in writing the

John S. Lott, secretary-treasurer of the Vigilantes. He wrote the Vigilante oath. Courtesy of Montana Historical Society.

circumstances of such an event, how frail is his memory of the long ago!

Davis always said he was sure the men above-named were at the meeting, but he could not be certain as to the other four. They were Alder Gulch men, of course. He continues, "The question arose as to how we could organize and this man from California suggested he had the oath, and told us what the particulars were and how the committee was organized in California."

Paris S. Pfouts wrote his memoirs years after these stirring scenes were closed and long after he had left Montana for good. He is indefinite as to details in important particulars. Referring to a meeting subsequent to the one held during the Ives trial, he says:

An oath of secrecy was administered to all and a plan of organization discussed. I and Colonel Sanders were for immediate and decisive action, but no conclusion was definitely arrived at. We continued our meetings and in the course of three or four days the number was increased to about 50, and all among the best and most reliable citizens of Virginia City, and in the mining camps surrounding it, when they resolved upon selection of a president or "chief."

If this was the meeting in the Fox house, a conclusion was definitely arrived at, although essentials in the way of organization were yet to be determined and officers were yet to be elected. It is pretty clear that before the meeting adjourned it was determined to act with the utmost expedition; and to that end those present were directed to proceed at once with the organization of companies. That same night a company was organized at Junction, of which Davis was captain.

[1] Harold Axford (Ed.), *Four Firsts for a Modest Hero, The Autobiography of Paris Swazy Pfouts* (Helena: Grand Lodge of Montana A.F. & A.M., 1968), p. 98.

Neil Howie and John Fetherstun, two Vigilantes. Howie (right) was called "bravest of the brave" and was a leading figure among the Vigilantes. Courtesy of Montana Historical Society.

Nor did Lott and Williams wait. Whether the plan upon which the organization was effected was agreed upon in Fox's blue house or not, the next day saw union in Nevada City, for on that day the famous "oath" now in the archives of the State Historical Society at Helena was drawn up and signed, and doubtless the signers were the 24 who went upon the "Deer Lodge Scout."

It is here inserted:

We the undersigned uniting ourselves in a party for the laudible purpos of arresting thievs & murderers & recovering stollen propperty do pledge ourselves upon our sacred honor each to all others & solemnly swear that we will reveal no secrets, violate no laws of right & never desert each other or our standard of justice so help us God as witness our hand & seal this 23 of December A D 1863.

It is my belief that this extraordinary document was written by John S. Lott, and my information is that he said he wrote it; if he said so, he did. The penmanship is very like that employed by him in letters he wrote to me. That it was hurriedly done and under stress of emergency is evident enough. Although Lott wrote it, he did not sign it; there is a vacant space for a signature which was not made at the head of the column—the customary (LS) following a signature in a document of importance stands alone. Immediately below is James Williams's (LS). Next in order are the signatures of 23 others. Seven of the signers at least were on the Ives expedition: James Williams, J. S. Daddow, Chas. Brown, E. Morse, Thos. Baume, Wm. Clark, and W. Palmer. Lott did not go upon either expedition. His presence was needed more in Nevada.

The enrollment of men in Vigilante units or companies proceeded at once; there were companies at Summit, Highland,

Virginia City, Adobetown, Junction, and five at Nevada City—always the staunchest stronghold. Within a week probably 1,500 men were enrolled as Vigilantes. Within this period the machinery for operation contained in the "Regulations and Bye Laws" was adopted. Differing from the Nevada City document, this one was written by an expert penman and it shows care and thought in its preparation. (But for binding force, pledged fidelity, and solemn determination, I, in imitation of Mark Twain, will back the illiterate Nevada compact against anything in the books!)

This important document first appeared in print in Hoffman Birney's *Vigilantes:*[2]

REGULATIONS AND BYE LAWS

This committee shall consist of a President or Chief, an Executive Officer, Secretary, Treasurer, Executive Committee, Captains and Lieutentants of Companies and such gentlemen of known worth and integrity as the Captains, Lieutenants, and other officers enumerated above may deem worthy of being made members.

The President shall be the supreme ruler of the Committee, shall reside in Virginia City, and shall have power to appoint Captains to raise Companies wherever and whenever he deems the interest of the Committee require the same, to call together the Executive Committee whenever the same should be convened to order the arrest of any suspicious or guilty person, to preside at all meetings whenever present, and to have such other powers as would naturally devolve upon one occupying his position.

A majority of votes of the Executive Committee shall constitute an election for President, and he shall hold his office until his successor is appointed and accepts the position.

The Executive Officer shall have the government and control of

[2]Hermann Hoffman Birney, *Vigilantes* (Philadelphia: Penn. Publishing Co., 1929).

Oath taken by the Vigilantes in Fox's blue house, December 23, 1863. Courtesy of Montana Historical Society.

all Captains, Lieutenants, and Companies, shall see that all orders of the Chief and Executive Committee are duly executed, shall have the selection of all persons sent out upon any expedition by the Executive Committee and choose a leader for the same and in case of the death or absence of the chief shall assume the duties of the office of President, until a new President is chosen.

The Secretary shall keep a correct record of all things proper to be written, the names of the Chief, Executive Officer, Secretary, Treasurer, Executive Committee, and the names of Captains and Lieutenants of Companies.

The Treasurer shall receive all monies belonging to the Committee, keep a true account of the same and pay them out again upon orders of the Executive Committee attested by the Secretary.

The Executive Committee shall consist of seventeen members, to wit: The President, Executive Officer, Treasurer, Secretary of the Committee, four persons to be selected from Virginia City, three from Nevada, one from Junction, one from Highland, one from Pine Grove, two from Summit, and one from Bivins Gulch, any eight of whom shall constitute a quorum.

It shall be the duty of the Executive Committee to legislate for the good of the whole Committee—to try all criminals that may be arrested, to pass upon all accounts that may be presented, and if just to order the same paid by the Treasurer and to take a general supervision of all criminal acts that may be committed within this Territory or come under their notice.

The Captains of Companies may be appointed by the President or the Executive Officer, who shall hold their offices until elected by the Companies themselves, every Captain shall have power to appoint one or more Lieutenants—the Captains and Lieutenants shall have the power to recruit their companies from men of integrity living in their midst, and when any one Company outside of Virginia City numbers over fifty effective men a division should be made and two companies formed from the same and officers elected from each.

It shall be the duty of members to attach themselves to some

48

company and whenever any criminal act shall come to their knowledge to inform his Captain or Lieutenant of the same, when the officers so informed shall call together the members of his Company, (unless the Company has chosen a committee for such purpose) when they shall proceed to investigate the case, and elicit the facts and should the said company conclude that the person charged with any offense should be punished by the committee, the Captain or Lieutenant will first take steps to arrest the Criminal and then report the same with proof to the Chief who will thereupon call a meeting of the Executive Committee and the judgment of such Executive Committee shall be final.

The only punishment that shall be inflicted by this Committee is DEATH.

The property of any person executed by this Committee shall be immediately seized upon and disposed of by the Executive Committee for the purpose of paying the Expenses of the Committee, and should the persons executed have creditors living in this Territory it shall be the duty of the Committee to first pay the Expenses of the Committee and Execution & Funeral Expenses, afterwards to pay the residue over to some one for the benefit of said creditors.

After the adoption of the "Regulations and Bye Laws" the captains and lieutenants elected Paris S. Pfouts, president; James Williams, executive officer; and John S. Lott, secretary and treasurer of the committee. While a prosecutor was not provided for, the captains and lieutenants, desiring to acknowledge the valiant conduct and inestimable services of Mr. Sanders, elected him prosecuting officer.

Perhaps it would be more accurate to say that the selection of Williams as executive officer was confirmed by the captains and lieutenants, for the fact seems to be that he was chosen as commanding officer in the field contemporaneously with the execution of the Nevada compact. At that time no other man was suggested for that perilous position. Williams said it was a job no one would covet, but if elected he would do the best he could. Once, asked how he came to be chosen leader, he answered, "There were a good many people there from Colorado, and they had an idea that I had some leather in me, I guess."

CHAPTER FOUR

The Power of the Road Agents Broken

*Capture, trial, and hanging of Yager and Brown. Astounding dis-
closure by Brown that Sheriff Henry Plummer was chief of the road
agents. Plummer, Stinson, and Ray hanged January 10, 1864.
More villains hanged.*

WITH CAPTAIN WILLIAMS chosen as the leader of the Vigilantes, steps were taken to hunt down the remaining "roughs."
In the "Deer Lodge Scout," Dimsdale gives us in vigorous language the background of the expedition which set forth and
fixes the date of its departure from Nevada City.

Almost instantly after the commencement of the organization of
the Vigilante Committee, it was determined that the pursuit of the
miscreants—the comrades of Ives—should be commenced and maintained with relentless earnestness, which should know no abatement
until the last blood-stained murderer had paid the penalty of his
crimes by death on the gallows; or had escaped the retribution in
store for him by successful flight to other countries.

Twenty-four men were mustered, whose equipment consisted of
arms, ammunition, and the most modest provision for the wants of
the inner man that could possibly be conceived sufficient. The vol-

unteers formed a motley group; but there were men enough among them of unquestioned courage, whom no difficulty could deter and no danger affright. They carried, generally, a pair of revolvers, a rifle or shotgun, blankets and some rope. Spirits were forbidden to be used.

The leader of the party was one of those cool, undaunted, and hardy men, whose career had been marked by honesty of purpose and fearlessness concerning the consequences of any just or lawful action, and to whom society owes a large debt for perils and hardships voluntarily undergone for the salvation of the lives and property of the people of this Territory, and for the punishment of wrong-doers.

Charles Beehrer, one of the most useful members of the expedition, has cast some interesting side lights upon the Dimsdale narrative.[1] From what he says, Williams must have furnished horses for that expedition as he did for the one which arrested Ives; and he speaks repeatedly of Williams being in command. He mentions Palmer, Daddow, Morse, Charles Brown, Louis Hooker, and Luther Seebold as members of the party. Hooker was the man who signed his surname only to the Nevada compact; the signature is almost illegible. Seebold, Beehrer says, "was a highly educated German gentleman," and Charley Brown, "that was not his real name," was in fact a nobleman. He was at one time a page at the Bavarian court and "was one of the boys that rode horses when the queen took a ride."

Beehrer says the party took with them Long John, who had "turned State's evidence" at the Ives trial, to identify the highwaymen. If so, where was John when the party met Red? The purpose of the expedition was to capture Alex Carter, supposed to be at Deer Lodge, and such of the road agents as

---

[1] Thomas J. Dimsdale, *The Vigilantes of Montana* (Helena: State Publishing Company, n.d.), pp. 263–271.

might be found with him, there being also a reasonable expectation of finding outlaws along the Big Hole River.

That the journey would be a hard one was foreseen, but the difficulties encountered were not within any one's contemplation. Be reminded that the journey was by saddle animals, which could not be expected to cover more than six miles an hour at best. The poor creatures, subsisting wholly upon grass pawed from under the deep snow, were not able to travel at that speed. The men were ill clad for the weather which grew increasingly severe, and they had little to eat. With insufficient blankets, a comfortable night's sleep could not be had. The story is one of continuous hardships—nearly two weeks of it.

The first camp was made on the Big Hole River about eight miles from present Twin Bridges, near the site of the Pennington bridge; the next day, by reason of deep snow upon the McCarty Range, the river was followed to a point near Camp Creek, where the night was spent. On the next day, despite the growing severity of the weather, a scouting party was sent across the river and up Glendale Creek where it was known the road agents had maintained a camp, but the effort was fruitless. The party resumed its journey to Deer Lodge, beating a trail in the snow on the divide between the Big Hole River—the summit of the main range of the Rockies—and the Silver Bow Creek. Crossing the "Hump," the Deer Lodge divide, a red-haired, red-whiskered man passed the Vigilantes along the freshly broken trail. It was Erastus Yager, "Red," who had killed two horses taking a message—"Git up and dust and lie low for black ducks"—from Brown, corresponding secretary of Plummer's band, to the road agents in Deer Lodge. None of the party knew Red. If any conversation passed between him and any of them, the information he gave was misleading.

Every precaution was taken to avoid alarming the road agents that were supposed to be in the little town; the plan was to take them by surprise. Needless to say the culprits had heeded the warning and fled. When Williams and his men found they had been tricked and the messenger who had conveyed the warning had been in their power, they were enraged and disgusted. The party remained in Deer Lodge for two days, principally to permit their worn-out horses to recuperate, to say nothing of their own need for rest. While some of the party thought the road agents might be hiding in the nearby country, the general opinion was that they had fled to the Bitterroot, which was the case.

The cold was increasing, and there seemed no alternative but to return, leaving further pursuit of the outlaws until later; so the disgusted and dispirited Vigilantes began to retrace the way. The return trip was more difficult than the first. On the main range the snow was 18 inches deep, a trackless waste. Williams said, "I never saw such weather, nothing like it."

Physical suffering is not conducive to thinking, but during the long ride the Captain was revolving in his mind the occurrences of the last ten days; and what had seemed a well-founded surmise ripened into a certainty—that the outlaws had perfected a smooth-working and effective organization. How else account for the warning so speedily conveyed to Deer Lodge?

The messenger, he determined, must be pursued and captured at any cost. This proved to be a decision of far-reaching importance. Finally the party reached the Beaverhead Rock; it was snowing heavily, night close on. Camp was made, but there was no firewood except willows, and dry willows were scarce. The food was low. A few horses were tethered, the rest turned loose. The next morning ushered in a blizzard, and the men's sufferings increased. To make matters worse the horses, which had been turned out to forage, drifted away in the storm and it was no small task to gather them. Almost the entire day was spent in this endeavor and in a struggle to keep from freezing.

"It is darkest just before dawn," and Fortune now smiled upon them. The party had but reached the road leading from Bannack to Virginia City when two horsemen were observed approaching. Tom Baume, in the lead, called upon them to throw up their hands. X. Beidler, one of the two, recognized Baume's voice and laughed. He said, "You might as well kill a man as scare him to death!"

The two, Beidler explained, himself and his friend, Andy Lewis, were on the way from Bannack to Virginia City. He had left Virginia, on the day after the hanging of Ives, to assist the Kiskadden freight train, which was found to be in distress at the Hole-in-the-Rock on the Salt Lake Road; his mission accomplished he was on his way home. Williams was pleased to see Beidler; the two were great friends. "What are you out on?" X. asked, and, when the object of the expedition was explained, he said he thought Red would be found at the Rattlesnake Ranch (on the way to Bannack); Stinson was there.

The Captain at once called for volunteers to go with him to arrest that swift messenger; all offered to go. Selecting seven men, the Captain directed the rest to go to Dempsey's and await his return, while he and his seven set out for Rattlesnake Ranch. At midnight they reached the Oliver & Co. stage station at Stone's ranch, where fresh horses were secured, and, after a short rest, pushed on the remaining 20 miles to Rattlesnake Ranch. Arriving there, Williams with two others sought to enter the house which was occupied by Buck Stinson and Ned Ray, who, as deputy sheriffs, had a prisoner in charge. Seeing Williams, to him "an ominous sight," Stinson appeared at the door with a drawn pistol, but, as he looked into the muzzles of pistols held by the Captain's companions, he concluded to be peaceful.

Red was found in a wickiup a short distance up Rattlesnake Creek, arrested, disarmed, and told he was to go to Virginia City. He went along quietly, cheerfully. During the long ride to Dempsey's he was not given any intimation as to the cause of his arrest, but he seemed to sense it. Indeed, he expected death when he met the Vigilantes on the Deer Lodge divide.

The main party had been at Dempsey's two days when the posse arrived there with Red. To the Captain's pleasure, but not to his surprise, the faithful and courageous Beidler was there. X. was not going to miss being in at the death! Placing Red in charge of men who had enjoyed sleep, the Captain and his companions ate supper and went to bed; but not until the Captain was informed that another important person was at Dempsey's—Brown. "Keep an eye on him," said the Captain.

After breakfast Red was taken by the Captain to a room and accused of being a road agent. He denied it."

"Why, then," said the Captain, "did you take a message to those fellows at Deer Lodge?"

Red answered that he had stopped at Dempsey's on his way to Deer Lodge and Brown had asked him to take a letter to Aleck Carter, and he had done so. Taking Red with him, the Captain called the party together and had Brown brought to the meeting. The two men were accused. Red again admitted carrying a letter written by Brown to Carter. Brown's manner showed his character; he was a sneaking, groveling, cowardly villain. Red, on the other hand, was a bold, straightforward man. Williams was a rare judge of human nature. As his brother John said, "if he got a chance to study a man for a short time, he seemed to know all about him."

It did not take him long to estimate the two men before

him. Brown, he perceived, though sly, was weak, without courage; he would break down under examination. Red, if he found himself entrapped, would likely confess; his disposition was to be frank. Brown was rattled, Red cool, as the conversation proceeded. The Captain decided to examine the men separately, and this was done. Their stories conflicted. As was anticipated, Brown's explanations were confused and highly incriminatory as to both himself and Red. On the other hand, Red attempted to maintain his original story, but he was not a good liar; he fell into inextricable inconsistencies and explanations. Be it said to the credit of the Vigilantes that no modern "third degree" methods were employed, neither force nor threats were resorted to.

The morning passed. After the noonday meal the entire party was called together upon the bridge over the Stinkingwater (Ruby) River. The Captain told his men they had heard "all about it" and each should vote according to his conscience. All who favored hanging should step to the right side of the bridge, those who favored letting them go should step to the left. The Captain stepped to the right, and the entire command followed him. The prisoners were informed they were to be taken to Virginia City, and eight men were detailed to take them to Laurin's, there to await the rest. In about two hours the detail with the prisoners reached Laurin; the Captain with the main party arrived at sundown. The Captain, worn from exertions and loss of sleep, lay down in the "parlor" of the tavern to rest, and soon passed into the arms of Morpheus.

The prisoners lay down in the barroom and slept. While the captain and the prisoners slept, the Vigilantes, who always reserved the right to express their own opinions, got to discussing the danger of taking Red and Brown to Alder Gulch for execution.

"Virginia City is really the headquarters of that gang. They

Hangman's Tree, Helena, Montana. Hanging of Joseph Wilson and Arthur L. Compton, April 27, 1870. Courtesy of Montana Historical Society.

know now we've got Red and Brown. They may give us a battle and that means bloodshed. More innocent men may be killed," said one, likely Beidler.

"We'd better hang them right here and be done with it," said another.

These expressions having reflected the concensus of opinion, at ten o'clock the Captain was awakened and informed of the judgment of his associates. After brief reflection, he agreed. Decision reached, as was customary with him, he acted swiftly. Red and Brown were awakened; perhaps the tenseness of the situation apprised Red that death was near; his confession was forthcoming. He told a Vigilante he was going to be hanged, that he knew all about the gang, and there were men in it who deserved hanging more than he did; he would die happy if he could see them hanged. Being apprised of this, Williams told Red his doom was sealed; but he would do a great service to mankind by disclosing what he knew. Red said he would do it.

His story was committed to writing. He began by giving his captors the astounding information that Henry Plummer, the sheriff, was the organizer and chief of the road agents; Bill Bunton was second in command; Brown was corresponding secretary; Ives had been a roadster, as were Stinson, deputy sheriff, Kinner, Marshland, Wagner, Carter, Graves, Shears, Cooper, Zachary, Parish, Lane ("Club-foot George"), and others. Boone Helm and Haze Lyons were roadsters and telegraph men. Ned Ray, deputy sheriff, was council keeper at Bannack. Dimsdale gives the list.

The confessions being finished, the execution took place; it was a weird scene, the suspension of the two road agents from the limbs of cottonwood trees in the darkness of near midnight, the only light being afforded by flickering candle lanterns. When the bodies were still, there was affixed to the back of Yager a paper bearing this legend: "Red! Road Agent and Messenger," and to the back of the other man a paper saying: "Brown! Corresponding Secretary."

The bodies hung there, a warning to all beholders for several days.

The deed done, the Vigilantes took a horse; and, upon arriving in Nevada City, went silently to bed. Williams was up betimes for a conference with Lott. The two went immediately to Virginia to report the information Williams had to impart. Pfouts called a meeting of the captains and lieutenants of the companies, inviting the presence of other leaders in the movement, for that night. Congratulations were showered upon Williams and his men; formal approval was given the selection of Pfouts as president, Williams as executive officer, Lott as secretary and treasurer, Sanders as prosecutor. A "Ferreting Committee" was appointed with the executive officer as chairman with full power to expend the moneys received by the treasurer. It was resolved that the executive officer proceed forthwith in the work of exterminating Henry Plummer's road agent band, and the meeting adjourned.

Williams moved with speed, but with caution, laying his plans; secrecy was essential. Within three days, with the president's approval, he dispatched Lott with three trustworthy men, Richard McLaren being one, to Bannack with instructions to enlist in the Vigilante movement strong men known to be in sympathy with it, and forthwith to hang Plummer, Stinson, Ray, and such others as the Bannack men might find to be members of Plummer's band. On January 10, 1864, Plummer, Stinson, and Ray were hanged simultaneously upon a scaffold Plummer had erected for others. The next day "Dutch John" Wagner was executed. He was a savage and bloodthirsty outlaw, captured under extraordinary circumstances by Neil

Grave of "Sheriff" Henry Plummer and Hangman's Gulch, Bannack, Montana. Courtesy of Montana Historical Society.

Howie, "the bravest of the brave," acting alone at first but aided later by John Fetherstun. Executed along with him was Pizanthia, "The Greaser."

Virginia City was a large camp, filled with saloons, hurdy-gurdy houses, and brothels, and hiding places were many. On January 13 the executive committee determined to capture at the same time, if possible, six men who were known to be Plummer's chief men in the Alder Gulch settlement. They were Boone Helm (robber, murderer, and cannibal), Jack Gallagher, Frank Parish, Haze Lyons, Club-foot George, and William Hunter. It had been ascertained that these men were then in Virginia City. Williams acted with characteristic energy. During the night a cordon of 250 men was thrown about the city with orders to permit anyone who chose to enter, but to allow no one to leave without written authority.

The captains of the companies at Junction, Nevada, Fairweather (in which Virginia City was located), Pine Grove, Highland, and Summit districts were directed to be in Virginia City at ten o'clock in the morning of January 14 with their companies in full force; the idea was to demonstrate the power of the Vigilantes as well as to execute the six road agents.

Morning presented a fearsome sight to the outlaws and their sympathizers; the tense air of excitement which pervaded the entire camp may easily be imagined. Miners up and down the gulch, anticipating something equal to a Roman holiday, came to the city, but many having good excuses wanted to leave. President Pfouts appointed A. B. Davis, captain of the Junction company, "pass master," and that zealous but careful man issued passes to a considerable number authorizing them to quit the city. Bill Hunter left without a pass. When he saw armed men "on every eminence and vantage point round the city," he knew it was time to go and made his escape by crawling down a drain ditch, being badly frozen before he finally got away. He won a respite only. The other five were soon captured and, in sight of the hundreds of armed Vigilantes and thousands of spectators, were hanged simultaneously from a beam which ran across the center of an unfinished building upon the northeast corner of Wallace and Van Buren streets. The building still stands and to this day the beam is an object of great interest in the ancient capital. The moral effect of this

Sun setting over road agents' graves on top of Boot Hill, Virginia City, Montana. By Michael J. Gordon, Virginia City, Montana.

spectacular blow was tremendous. The power of the road agents was broken, but the power of individual outlaws to work mischief remained.

The committee determined to capture next those who had fled from Deer Lodge to the Bitterroot. Williams told me Dimsdale had the history of these expeditions "about right," and I shall follow his narration pretty closely. On January 15th, Williams with 20 men, including his trusted lieutenant X. Beidler, and a number of those who with him had suffered the hardships and disappointments of the Deer Lodge scout, set forth. Steve Marshland was captured and executed at Clarke's Big Hole Ranch on January 16th. Bill Bunton was found at Deer Lodge, tried, and convicted. He was told that he was to be hanged, and if he had any business to attend to, he had better get someone to do it. Thereupon Bunton gave his gold watch to his partner, saying that the rest of his property should pay his debts. Only two weeks before, he had acquired his interest in the saloon, which he was running by gambling.

At the place of execution he was asked if he had anything to say, to which he answered that he should like to have his neck broken.

"All I want," he said, "is a mountain three hundred feet high to jump off."

He said he would give the signal himself, which he did. "One, two, three, here goes it," he said, jumping to practically instantaneous death. X. Beidler was detailed to remain for the purpose of collecting and disposing of Bunton's property and paying his debts. "Tex," found with Bunton, was tried; but as the evidence against him was not conclusive, he was permitted to go. This was the invariable rule with the Vigilantes. In this case a great mistake was made, for Tex was an outlaw, a highwayman.

Headboards of road agents' graves on Boot Hill, Virginia City, Montana. Courtesy of Montana Historical Society.

The posse then made its difficult way down the river to Hellgate where it was known that Carter and others of the road agents would be found. The snow was deep and the weather was very cold. In crossing the Deer Lodge River, some of the horses broke through the ice, and one of the party nearly lost his life. On the first day after leaving Deer Lodge, the party made its way through snow two or three feet deep. All the way the traveling was difficult because of the deep snow. As indicating the hazards of the expedition, it may be mentioned that in driving the horses into camp one of them broke his leg in a badger hole; another by falling in a hole stripped the skin from his hind leg. The first animal was shot, the second left until the expedition's return. When the party eventually reached the vicinity of Hellgate, the Captain sent a party ahead to reconnoiter. When within a short distance of Hellgate, the Captain dismounted his party and awaited the return of the scouting party, which returned with information respecting the lay of the land. When ready, the entire party rushed into the settlement upon the dead run, taking the inhabitants by surprise. Skinner was in his saloon and, at the command of the Vigilantes, threw up his hands and was bound with ropes. Carter, who had been running about the town with a pistol in his hand a short time before, after shooting Johnny Cooper, was found lying upon a lounge in a drunken condition. He was bound likewise. Cooper was found in his house wounded in three places. He was arrested and put in charge of the guard.

The same night eight men were dispatched to Baron O'Keeffe's in the "Coriacan Defile" to capture Bob Zachary; O'Keeffe was entertaining Zachary unaware of the character of his guest. Zachary was taken to Hellgate to await the judgment of the committee. Conversation with this road agent elicited the fact that George Shears, horse thief and road agent, probably was at Van Dorn's in the Bitterroot valley. A party was immediately dispatched to capture that miscreant. Arriving at that destination, Van Dorn was asked if George Shears was in the house, and being told that he was, and that the party might enter, Shears was found in his room, knife in hand. But he surrendered quietly, and, being advised that he was about to die, he confessed his guilt, saying that he knew he would have "to go up sometime," but had thought he could "run another season."

The coolness of this youth of 21 was remarkable. On being taken to the barn, where the hangman's rope had been thrown over a beam, he was ordered to walk up a ladder in order that a sufficient drop might be had. This he did, and, being seated on the beam, said, as if it was an ordinary affair: "Gentlemen, I am not used to this business, never having been hung before. Shall I jump off or slide off?"

He was advised to jump off if he desired a speedy death. "All right," he said, "Good bye!" and jumped.

In the meantime a company of three, headed by the "Old Man," probably Clark, was on its way to Fort Owen in pursuit of William Graves, "Whiskey Bill," road agent. He had frequently threatened that he would kill any Vigilante on sight, but the old man "got the drop on him" and Graves surrendered. He was executed upon a nearby tree.

At Hellgate Carter and Skinner were first tried, found guilty, and executed. The hanging, shortly after midnight, was a typical Vigilante execution. The Vigilantes knew their psychology; a great fire was built, throwing its weird light over the scene. Two poles were placed over a corral fence, the ends at the ground secured, and to the other ends the ropes were tied. The bodies of these road agents, swinging from the ends of the poles, gave stern warning to other malefactors.

The next morning the party came in with Zachary; and, after his trial was concluded, he and Cooper, who had also been found guilty, were hanged from the same poles which had served as a gallows for Skinner and Carter.

This work done, the captain, after dispatching a party to the Pend O'Reille Indian Reservation to get Cooper's horses, wended his way homeward, picking up Beidler, who had settled up Bunton's affairs at Deer Lodge. Arriving in Alder Gulch, the party reported its doings, which, being made known to the inhabitants of the gulch, enabled all except certain of the roughs to enjoy life with a greater feeling of security.

It will be recalled that Bill Hunter had escaped by crawling down a drain at the time Club-foot George, Boone Helm, Jack

Gallagher, Frank Parish, and Haze Lyons were captured. It was ascertained that Hunter had fled into the Gallatin Valley and Williams at once dispatched A. B. Davis, John S. Lott, John S. Bagg, and Richard S. McLaren to capture and execute the fugitive. On the way the party in charge of Davis was reinforced by Charles Leyendecker and companion, whose name is lost. It is interesting to note that the posse spent the first night out at Slade's place on Slade Creek. "Old Jimmy" Boner, once an employee under Slade on the Overland, was cook. Boner was for many years a respected citizen on the Meadow Creek settlement in Madison County. Davis says, "They gambled all night at Slade's and the next morning we were told by the hostler that Mrs. Slade had won $1,200."

After a severe journey through deep snow, Hunter was found in a cabin not far from where Manhattan now stands and was summarily executed on February 3, 1864.

Williams, in the exercise of his duties as executive officer, was now to meet again an old acquaintance, Captain Joseph A. Slade.

CHAPTER FIVE

The Strange and Tragic Story of Joseph Alfred Slade

A Montana version of Dr. Jekyll and Mr. Hyde. A born leader, brave, competent, and a charmer when sober, a dangerous and vicious man when drinking. He dies by the hangman's noose.

IN THE HISTORY of the West there is not a more extraordinary life story than that of Joseph Alfred Slade. The period produced exceptional individuals; but a combination of circumstances affecting an unusual temperament has set him apart as unique. He seems to have been an ordinary boy, sprung from an excellent family. His father, Charles Slade, was a native of England, a child coming to this country with his parents who settled in Alexandria, Virginia. There Charles grew to manhood, having acquired a common school education, together with habits of thrift and industry. In 1816, Charles, with his two brothers, Richard and Thomas, migrated to Illinois, settling along the Okaw River in what was then St. Clair County. They were pioneers in that locality. In 1819, Charles married a daughter of John Kane, a native of Virginia, who some years before had migrated to Ohio and then moved on to the locality in which the Slades lived. Mr. Kane became a wealthy and influential citizen, dying at his Illinois home at an advanced age in 1833.

Charles Slade engaged in merchandising and then added milling to his activities. He built the first mill of any pretentions in his part of Illinois, at Carlyle, a town founded by him. In 1824, the legislature created Clinton county, designating Carlyle the county seat, provided the citizens of that village would donate to the county for public use not less than 20 acres of land. Charles Slade and Mary D. Slade, his wife, at once donated the ground. Mr. Slade was then one of the most prosperous and popular citizens of southern Illinois. He was elected to the legislature in 1820 and again in 1826. President Andrew Jackson appointed him U.S. marshal for Illinois in 1829, the year Joseph Alfred Slade was born. Prior to 1830, Illinois had one representative in the lower house of Congress; after the census of that year reapportionment gave the state three. In the southern district five candidates entered the field for congressman: Mr. Slade; former Governor Ninian Edwards, one of the ablest and most brilliant men in the state; Col. Sidney Breese, afterward chief justice and later United States senator; and two others. At the ensuing election Mr. Slade won by a substantial majority, his nearest competitor being Governor Edwards. He took his seat in Congress on the first Monday of December, 1833. It is reported that he "sustained himself well, guarding the interests of his constituents and state with fidelity and ability." Upon the adjournment of the session, after attending to business in the departments in Washington and visiting relatives and friends at Alexandria, Mr. Slade, about July 1st, turned home. At Cincinnati he was striken with illness, partially recovered, resumed his journey, and was again stricken in Indiana, where he died at a roadside tavern, not far from Vincennes. Surviving him were his wife and five children, named William Henry, Charles Richard, Mary Kane, Joseph Alfred, and Maria Virginia.

His second son, Charles R. Slade, married a daughter of Judge Breese, but upon the outbreak of the Mexican War enlisted in the First Regiment of Illinois Foot Volunteers, Colonel Edward W. B. Newby commanding. Joseph Alfred, not to be outdone by his elder brother, enlisted in Company A of the same regiment, Captain Bond commanding. The army records show that Joseph A. Slade gave his age at the time of his enlistment, May 4, 1847, as 18 years. Upon the march to Mexico, Charles, then a quartermaster sergeant, fell sick, dying at Santa Fe.

Joseph served through the campaigns in Mexico with his regiment and returned with it, being honorably discharged as a private at Alton, Illinois, on October 16, 1848. Before he went to war, Joseph, hereafter to be referred to simply as Slade, was a quiet, well-behaved, inoffensive youth. He had not been long in the army before he showed his courage. N. P. Langford in this *Vigilante Days and Ways*,[1] relates that an officer, "distinguished for success in reconnoitre, strategy and surprise," requiring a dozen men of unquestioning daring and energy for a dangerous enterprise, selected Slade among the number. Slade was an efficient soldier whose acts always won the approbation of his commander.

After the young soldier, following his discharge from the army, returned to his home in Carlyle, he continued to hold the respect of the community for his excellent qualities. No record remains of the slightest criticism of his conduct prior to the fatal encounter which changed the course of his life. This

---

[1] Nathaniel Pitt Langford, *Vigilante Days and Ways* (Boston: J. G. Cupples Co., 1890).

grew out of a quarrel, leading to a fight with another man, during which his antagonist was killed. One account says Slade was 22 years of age, another that he was 26 at the time. From the meager information which has come down, it seems that his adversary was getting the better of the encounter when Slade made use of a rock; whether he flung it or used it as a hammer does not appear definitely. Clearly it was not murder—manslaughter at most. It is probable that had he stayed at home and stood trial he would have been acquitted. That any real effort was made to effect Slade's arrest is unlikely, although we find the statement here and there that the sheriff of Clinton County pursued him with a warrant for a number of years. The sheriff's heart could not have been in his task, for at least as early as 1859, likely before that, Slade was a famous man along the Oregon Trail, the main artery of travel from Missouri to the west. He returned to Carlyle for a visit in the spring of 1863. He was not arrested; indeed, he never was arrested for homicide, nor for any infraction of the law save disturbance of the peace. In weighing the probability of the stories of his personal killings, this fact should be kept in mind.

Regardless of whether the sheriff wanted to catch Slade, that misguided young man, immediately after the affray at Carlyle, fled across the Mississippi; and for a time his movements cannot be traced. It is said he lived among the Indians for a considerable period. Whether this is true or not, in the latter 50's he is seen engaged in freighting along the Oregon Trail, then a hazardous, exciting, and uncertain employment, becoming more hazardous as one went westward.

It is difficult for us now to visualize the conditions which obtained in the vast territory through which the Oregon Trail and the stage line, which came to be called the Overland, pass. The region was known in the 1850's and well into the

lls, Fargo & Co.'s station, Virginia City, Montana, 1865. Courtesy of Montana storical Society.

1860's as the Great American Desert. Confining this narrative to the route of the Overland stage line, after leaving the Missouri River and going westward, it ran through an unsettled savage country. Stage stations, lonely outposts of civilization, dotted this wilderness at intervals, approximately ten or twenty miles apart, depending upon the difficulty of the terrain. The names of Fort Kearney and Julesburg stand out before reaching Denver. At a station called Bijou, west of Julesburg, the trail divided, one line going southwest to Denver, the other going northerly from Denver. They both joined the one running westerly at Latham and Laporte. From the latter station the Overland ran by the stations of Boner, Virginia Dale, and

Gilbert at the west end of the South Pass. From this point Lander's Cutoff ran northwesterly through what became Wyoming to near Fort Hall, now near Pocatello, Idaho, and on to Fort Bridger, Salt Lake City, Carson City, Placerville, and Sacramento. Many of the stations along the Overland led a precarious existence; some were wiped out temporarily by Indians on the warpath. The terrain was rough, to say the least, for many miles; seemingly interminably long, and for considerable distances heavy sand had to be traversed; perilous hills and the Great Rocky Range had to be crossed. Practically the entire road was infested with warlike Indians.

Every man who earned his livelihood along the trail had to become an Indian fighter and Slade was one par excellence. Mark Twain, in *Roughing It,*[2] states: "It is said that in one Indian fight he killed three warriors with his own hand and afterwards cut their ears off and sent them, with his compliments, to the chief of the tribe." Root, in *The Overland Stage to California,*[3] repeats the story. Hearsay, of course, and possibly true; but this ear story arouses a suspicion: is it a throwback from the Jules episode, or did Slade have a penchant for cutting off ears?

Indian fighting was not the only strife in which the adventurous denizens of the frontier were likely to become embroiled. We are told that fighting was the order of the day. Men fought with fist, knife, pistol, at the drop of the hat, and even without that formality. The passing of the lie, flinging the unpardonable epithet, called for action. In a region without law, overrun by warlike Indians, horse thieves, and highwaymen, every man for his self-protection carried a pistol and

[2] Mark Twain, *Roughing It* (New York: Harper & Row, reprint of 1875 ed.).
[3] Frank A. Root and William Elsey Connelley, *The Overland Stage to California* (Topeka, Kansas: Published by the authors, 1901).

sought to become proficient in its use. Indiscriminate use of that weapon followed as a natural consequence. So the cool-headed man, with true eye, quick on the trigger, held superiority over those less gifted. Slade was highly gifted; none could draw quicker or shoot truer. Even at a later time, when intoxicated, he shot with remarkable accuracy. Probably he was quick-tempered, but if he was, he possessed the unusual faculty of being abnormally cool in anger or when laboring under excitement.

There is no doubt that he came through his freighting experiences a seasoned frontiersman, with the reputation of a first-class fighting man. From freighting to the more interesting employment of driving a stage was a logical graduation, a step by Slade not long delayed. His experience as a driver proved an essential part of his education in the activity in which he was soon to become so considerable a figure. It may be presumed that one with his innate executive ability, whether then realized by him or not, looked forward to promotion. That came with his appointment as the stage company's agent at Kearney, one of the most important points on the Overland. At whose special direction he was given the agency at Kearney seems obscure. The period was difficult for those operating the stage line. Bad management, thievery by employees and others had brought the company near to bankruptcy.

Fortunately for the company, the directors made a change in management. Instead of the man who had been superintendent, who it appears was honorable but inept in that particular activity, Benjamin Ficklin, a strong man thoroughly familiar with stage management and a good judge of men, was put in charge. There is a story that Slade was not unknown to Ficklin: that when the latter was in charge of the Pony Express, forerunner of the stage coaches from Independence West, he had with him the redoubtable Slade. Anyway one of the first acts of Ficklin was to remove Jules as station agent at Julesburg and to install Slade as superintendent of the Sweetwater Division, thus bringing upon himself and Slade the implacable hatred of Jules. While at Kearney, Slade had had the supervision over considerable territory. At that time he had earned the reputation of being coolheaded, fearless, and resolute.

The stage station which became famous as Julesburg was built early in 1859 on the south side of the Platte River, opposite the mouth of Lodge Pole Creek, and about one mile east of where Ft. Sedgwick, the starting point of the Bozeman Trail, was afterwards erected. The place derived its name from Jules Reni, a well known character, generally called "Old Jules" along the Platte. Jules had been an Indian trader in that region for a number of years, and must have borne the reputation of being a trustworthy man, for the stage company placed him in charge of the station which had been given his name. Julesburg soon became known as "the toughest town between the Missouri River and the mountains." It was a rendezvous for robbers, horse thieves, gamblers, and the free-booting crew that infested the stage line for many miles, east and west. Sudden death was not infrequent, injuries common from shooting or stabbing. Horse stealing was a common occurrence, and a favorite practice of the thieves was to run off the stock which, curiously enough, could be returned speedily for a reward through the kindly offices of Jules, the stage agent.

Exasperating as was the loss of its horses and the consequent expense, the company was most annoyed by the enforced delays and the impossibility of running its coaches on time under these conditions. And be it remembered that the company was under obligation to transport the mails promptly. Hay which the company bought would catch fire unaccountably, and a ranchman having hay for sale would, through the intervention of Jules, make a highly advantageous sale to the company. The stage was held up not infrequently and the passengers robbed. That the company's business was demoralized and eventually brought to the verge of bankruptcy does not excite wonder. It seems clear that Ficklin regarded Jules as a thief, an associate of thieves. Slade knew the conditions about Julesburg and he appreciated the dangers to be apprehended at that station. However, though he had grown used to peril, he was not careless of his safety.

With all its dangers it is pretty certain the opportunity strongly appealed to Slade. In the first place he hated a thief, and he detested a horse thief. In this day we can hardly appreciate how precious a horse was to a person's safety upon the plains, but the reason was that a horse was deemed the frontier man's most essential possession. At times a horse was worth a great deal more than the best firearm ever devised. A man set afoot in a howling wilderness infested with warlike Indians certainly was in deep trouble. Horse stealing became a capital crime. Moreover, in a business sense Slade was an honest man.

At once upon assuming the reins of authority, he gave warning that nothing must be allowed to interfere with the stage coaches, passengers, horses, or other property of the stage company. To emphasize the warning which was broadcast up and down the line, he said he "meant business."

Slade knew his problems. He must effect a complete organization of the physical properties of his company in order that passengers might be transported in safety and in such comfort as circumstances would permit and that the mail might go through on time. To accomplish this he must stop the depredation of the outlaws. He knew the medicine for the disease which was endemic along the Overland Trail from Julesburg to Rocky Ridge; and it was fear, and he determined to create a terror in his administration. That he did so, doubtless led to the general reputation which is to his discredit. Without an understanding of the conditions immediately in his face the conclusion might seem justified.

In principle, however, it may be argued that the end justified the means (if that argument is ever allowable), as it did with William T. Coleman and his Vigilantes of California, or with the highly moral Paris S. Pfouts, the patriotic hero Wilbur F. Sanders, and their followers in Montana. There comes, fortunately at long intervals, an emergency which demands extreme measures in the people's interest in a peace loving community which demanded law and order or its equivalent. It is true that Coleman led an organization, the famed Vigilantes of California; and Pfouts was the president of, and Sanders the prosecutor in and of, the Vigilantes of Montana. Both of these organizations were voluntary, pursuing the lawless equivalent of legal administration in their own hands. Slade essentially followed the same policy. He arrogated to himself a position equivalent to that of chief prosecutor, as well as executioner, with the aid of men who, virtually, if not actually, were his employees.

The Sweetwater Division, covering a distance of more than two hundred miles, was the most perilous along the entire line from Kearney, Nebraska, to Placerville, California. In addition to constant danger from hostile Indians it was infested with every sort of outlaw. The next division to the west, or more accurately to the northwest of the Sweetwater, was the Rocky Ridge, and it was next to the Sweetwater as a trouble maker. After a careful search of the records it does not seem possible to say just where the Sweetwater Division began and the Rocky Ridge Division ended, but it is pretty well established that the two covered perhaps 500 or 600 miles along the stage line. What that meant to one who must travel it in those early days when horse and foot power alone furnished locomotion can hardly be realized by those who have grown up under modern conditions.

Having arrived at Julesburg, the new agent rode up and down the road, keenly surveying every rod of it. He gave special attention to the stage stations, inspecting men, horses, harness, coaches, and the general equipment necessary to a stage line. His solicitude for the comfort and safety of the company's passengers was noteworthy.

Day and night Slade worked upon his job, striving to bring order out of the chaos which Jules had left; and he established what a mediaeval king would have called law and order, and, as above noted, in much the same fashion.

It was not long before he demonstrated that he "meant business." Hay belonging to the stage company burned, unaccountably. Slade bought a stack to replace it from a nearby ranchman. The stack was found to contain willows, brush, and the like. Slade chained the ranchman to a log near the stack, to which he set fire, threatening, when the fire got well under way, to throw log and man into the flames. Only upon the ranchman's promise to leave the country did Slade release him. The man left. Quickly following this, a stage was held up, the passengers robbed. Swiftly Slade, with a chosen few, pursued. The robbers were hanged to a gate post and left to hang. Whether two, three, or four is not essential now. A little later two horse thieves were hanged from the limb of a tree. Their bodies remained as a warning.

Slade did not permit any man, except a superior in the service, to challenge his authority. His word was law. He would fight with fist, knife, or pistol; and, according to Dimsdale, he did so. There is no record of his having killed personally while in charge of the Julesburg Division (unless Jules), although it is said that with two or three followers he would attack and put to death outlaws. It did not take much of this to quiet the Sweetwater Division. Now the stages went through on time. There might be delays on other divisions, but there were none on Slade's. He had restored order and guaranteed safety to honest men along his division in a few months. The horse thieves and most of the outlaws moved on to the Rocky Ridge Division.

But during this period came a collision with Old Jules with its far reaching results. This affair eventually did more than all else to brand Slade, perhaps forever, as a killer and a brute.

Ficklin, after investigation, determined that Jules had been stealing from the company and forced Jules to a settlement. Jules, resentful because he had been superseded by Slade, blamed him for some of Ficklin's acts. Slade, on his part, convinced of Jules's rascality, kept a keen watch upon him. One day he took away from Jules two horses claimed to belong to the stage company. Jules swore vengeance but bided his opportunity. It was not long coming. In the spring of 1860, Slade, out on an inspection trip, spent the night thirty miles westerly from Julesburg, with his friends James Boner and Phil James, the station keepers, two intelligent men, afterwards well known residents of Meadow Creek in Madison County, Montana.

Slade liked to stay with Boner and James. He found them pleasant companions; and most of the other stations, said Boner, "were kept by Frenchmen of a class that were not very agreeable, as they had a lot of Indians hanging around." Leaving his friends on the fateful morning, Slade forgot to take his knife and pistol. Never before had he done that, and never again did he forget them. That an encounter between Jules and Slade was expected by those conversant with affairs in the division is shown by the exclamation of Boner to his partner, "Phil, Slade has gone without his gun, and I'll just bet that

Jules shoots him if he gets a chance." When the coach arrived at a station, where, it appears, Old Jules was living, Slade saw one Tom Bryan with whom he held a conversation, the two sitting upon wagon-hubs. Old Jules saw them and observed that Slade was without his pistol. The conversation with Bryan concluded, Slade walked toward the little store, in which was the inevitable bar. Before he reached the door, Jules stepped out and commenced firing with a six-shooter; he put the six balls into Slade's body; Slade did not fall but walked around the house. Not satisfied, Jules ran into the house, from which he emerged a moment later with a shotgun loaded with buck-shot, and he emptied both barrels at Slade. Thinking he had finished his enemy, Jules fled to the Rocky Ridge country to be among his friends. That Slade was not killed seems mirac-ulous. The army surgeon at Fort Laramie, 167 miles distant, was summoned and reached the wounded man's bedside in record time. Boner and James arrived post-haste to nurse their friend. "The doctor picked out half a handful of lead from Slade," said Boner, "and yet, when he was hanged he carried several of Jules's bullets in him. I never saw a man so badly riddled as he was; he was like a sieve, and I do not see how he ever lived." Nor does anyone else understand how he lived. Jules's powder must have been weak. It is said, how credibly the writer does not avouch, that, as soon as he was able to be transported, Ficklin had him sent to St. Louis for treatment.

So thoroughly had Slade done his work that peace reigned in the Julesberg Division during his illness.

But conditions in the Rocky Ridge Division were giving superintendent Ficklin the gravest concern. The malefactors who had survived the Slade cleanup had congregated there, augmenting the outlaws who preceded them. That division was now worse than the Sweetwater ever had been. Ficklin perceived the remedy but hesitated to transfer Slade until his complete recovery. As soon as he thought Slade fit, Ficklin made him division-agent of Rocky Ridge. There is some indication that Slade also retained his sway over the Sweetwater. He had begun to enjoy, in fact to crave, the excitement of danger, and he entered upon his new task with a sort of fierce joy. For one thing Jules was there, protected by the mischiefmakers, and he was determined to make Jules pay.

That Slade's superiors approved of his methods in subduing the low element is certain. It is reported that Ben Holladay himself, owner of the Overland, told Slade that his policy of striking terror was the effectual way to afford protection to the company and those in its charge, and nothing could be more effective than the elimination of Jules. "Get that fellow Jules and let everybody know you got him." But he did not "get him" for over a year, according to E. M. Pollinger, once a driver along the Overland Trail.

Slade began a cleanup of the Rocky Ridge Division with characteristic energy. He now had a retinue of devoted followers who obeyed his orders with alacrity and zeal. In his first raid upon the desperadoes many were killed, stage horses were recovered in goodly numbers, and depredations upon the company's property ceased. But the outlaws were not willing to give up without a struggle. Congregating in the mountains, they planned a master stroke, the capture of the tyrant who had tumbled their world about them and who menaced their very existence.

Slade, having restored order upon his two divisions, sought a fixed abode. During his inspection trips he was attracted by the scenic beauty of a spot on Dale Creek, and here he established a station and his home. He called the station Virginia Dale in honor of his beauteous wife and, one may suppose, his youngest sister bearing the same name.

Now there was quiet along the Overland and it would seem

that Slade was lured into a state of false security. The story, repeated again and again as a fact, is that Slade was caught off his guard by a dozen of his enemies, was disarmed and taken to a lonely log cabin where he was kept prisoner, awaiting the arrival of the chiefs of the band who were to determine the manner of his end. (Was Jules in this?) Slade, cool and resourceful always, persuaded his captors that, as his escape was impossible, there was no reason why his wife should not come alone to see him and that it was permissible at least to allow him to tell her farewell and to give her directions respecting the property which would be hers after he was gone. This was arranged; Mrs. Slade came on horseback, apparently unarmed, and was permitted to enter the cabin by the only door it afforded. Presently she and Slade came forth, she with one six-shooter, he with two. The captors, upon command, raised their hands to the skies, while Mr. and Mrs. Slade mounted double and rode away.

Slade, who never forgot nor forgave, now determined to make an example of Jules. Orders were given to bring in Jules alive. Jules was brought in. Just what was the manner of his barbarous finish, from that day to this has been the subject of innumerable disputes. Slade let everyone know that he got him! The generally accepted version along the Overland is the story told in *Roughing It*. It is that when Slade's "myrmidons," as Mark Twain put it, brought in Jules, bound hand and foot, they tied him to the "snubbing-post" in the center of a corral. Slade examined his helpless victim with a devilish pleasure, and then went to bed, content to wait until morning before enjoying the pleasure of killing him. Jules spent the awful night, numb with cold and fear, tied to that snubbing-post; and when morning came, Slade, pistol-shot extraordinary, began the diabolical execution. His bullets nipped the victim's flesh here and there, then a finger disappeared, and only after

"Killing of Jules Reni by Slade," by Charles M. Russell. Courtesy of the Amon Carter Museum of Western Art, Fort Worth, Texas.

Jules had begged him time and time again to put him out of his misery did Slade end it; and then he let the body lie where it was for half a day, eventually assisting in the burial after cutting off Jules's ears for pocket pieces—souvenirs of the occasion!

Here is Boner's story: after shooting Slade, Jules absented himself for a long time, but eventually he turned up at Cold Spring station, announcing that when he again saw Slade he would finish him. Hearing that Jules was at Cold Spring, Slade armed two of his men, Scott and Hodges, with shotguns; and the three went to Cold Spring on the stage to capture Jules. At Cold Spring there was a combined station, trading post, and saloon, kept by a Frenchman named Sochet. Jules was in the building when the stage came in sight. Seeing Slade with the driver, Jules, protecting himself behind a corner of the house, began shooting; but Hodges and Scott, going opposite ways around the house, "got the drop on Jules," who was compelled to surrender—poor judgment on his part. Slade ordered his men to take Jules to the corral and to tie him to a post. This accomplished, Slade said to Jules, "You made me suffer, now I'll try to pay you for it." He then shot Jules in the arm and went in and took a drink. Then he came out and shot him again and went in and took another drink. He kept this up, alternating the shots with drinks, until Jules was dead and he himself was drunk, and then he cut off the dead man's ears and put them in his vest pocket.

Another version was told to the writer by the veracious "Gov." E. M. Pollinger, once a driver along the Overland, and later a superintendent of stage lines in Montana for Wells, Fargo & Co. Pollinger was in a position to learn the facts and he was a reliable man. "Slade simply had to get Jules," said Mr. Pollinger, "or quit the line. There was no other way out. Order in the division depended on Slade, and he could not enforce it while Jules was alive and defiant. You may not see it now, but it was plain enough then." Being unable to encounter Jules in person, Slade offered $500 for him alive, no reward if Jules were brought in dead. A number of men undertook the capture without success. Finally it was accomplished by Nelson Vaughan and John Frey after a hard fight in which Jules was wounded. Vaughan and Frey conveyed their captive, bound upon a pack-horse, to the station where Slade then was. But to their dismay, Jules died on the way in. Fearful of losing the reward, they tied Jules in a sitting position to the snubbing-post in the corral and told Slade they had his man. Slade said, "I supposed you had to kill him, and if you did you do not get any reward." They said, no, but he was hurt, for they captured him after a fight—"he's out in the corral." When Slade saw Jules he said, "the man is dead." They said, "He's only playing possum." Slade said, "I'll see whether he's playing possum," took out his knife and cut off an ear and, when Jules did not flinch, said, "that proves it, but I might just as well have the other ear," and took that.

Another says Vaughan cut off the ears and gave them to Slade. Anyhow, Slade had the ears, which seemed to possess a fascination for him. He carried them as pocket pieces with his money. At length these gruesome objects appeared tanned and pliable like leather. He did not know these playthings were leading him to the gallows; they were, unsuspected by him, the tokens of Nemesis. After the finish of Jules, however it was, every bizarre occurrence along the road in Slade's territory, especially of a homicidal nature, was credited to him. And apparently, he had no disposition to deny anything; it fitted in with his policy of terrorism. It is easy to visualize the picture of the young and then untraveled Mr. Clemens on his way to become private secretary to his brother, newly appointed secretary of the Territory of Nevada, sitting high on the stagecoach beside the loquacious driver who, as the coach rattled through the sagebrush wastes and the canyons along the Overland, regaled the young man with hair-raising tales of the mighty Slade. The perspicacious Mr. Clemens did not swallow it all without straining. It was a good story and he proceeded to write it. In his inimitable style he reduced what he termed "this mass of overland gossip" to a straightforward narrative. Most subsequent stories of Slade's activities along the Overland are based largely upon *Roughing It*. But the dismal fact is that the other writers, lacking the fine discrimination of the masterwriter, failed to make distinctions and state as history that which Mark Twain either directly or by implication ascribed to gossip or wrote as mixed fact and legend.

Mark Twain relates that he took breakfast with Slade at one of the stage stations:

The most gentlemanly appearing, quiet and affable officer we had yet found along the route in the Overland company's service, was the person who sat at the head of the table, at my elbow. Never youth suffered and shivered as I did when I heard them call him Slade. . . . Here right by my side was the actual ogre, who, in fights and brawls, had taken the lives of twenty-six human beings, or all men lied about him. . . . He was so friendly and so gentle spoken that I warmed to him in spite of his awful history. . . . And to this day I can remember nothing remarkable about Slade except that his face was rather broad across the check bones, and that the cheek bones were low and the lips peculiarly thin and straight.

He expected to hear about him later. (And he did.) When the stage was ready to go this agent "came out to the coach and saw us off, first ordering certain rearrangements of the mail bags for our comfort."

It is regrettable that Mark Twain, with his excellent descriptive faculty, did not pay more attention to Slade's personal appearance. Had he done so, various descriptions in print and even in the moving pictures of a later day perhaps would not have appeared. Pictures of a gangling, savage appearing, six-footer, of demoniacal mien likely would not have appeared. Although if there is anything new or strange in such imaginings, amounting to caricature, the reputation of Slade seems to have suffered beyond his deserts. "He weren't no saint," but most of this trash has been unfair, to say nothing more of it. He was, according to those who knew him intimately, under rather than over five feet eight inches in his boots, round rather than square of build, weighing about 150 pounds. His frame was covered with muscles of steel. He struck a powerful blow: often, the storywriters say, he knocked prostrate a large man with a single blow. The writer's most reliable informant said "his eyes were blue, with lots of fun in them, but in anger or excitement they seemed to turn jet black." Usually clean-shaven, his complexion was ruddy, his hair a reddish brown. After the death of Jules, Slade was at the summit of his power. He was the virtual dictator from Julesburg to Pacific Junction. It was of this period which Dimsdale had in mind when he said: "From Kearney, west, he was feared a great deal more than the Almighty."

Now, every sort of homicidal exploit was attributed to Slade. Stories, heretofore told of famous killers, were attributed to him. One was that at Rocky Ridge one morning Slade observed a man who had offended him some days before. Turning to this friend he said, "It is a good twenty yards shot; I'll clip the third button on his coat," which he did and a funeral followed. Another was that a saloon keeper had angered the great man who, a few days later, called at the saloon and asked for brandy. The saloon keeper turned around to get the article and, when he presented it, found himself gazing into the muzzle of a six-shooter. The next instant he was lying on the floor a dead man. This story never was verified and it is so at variance with Slade's methods as to be unworthy of belief.

One, coming from a respectable source, was that when Slade was wagon-boss of a freight team on the way to Salt Lake, he, drunk, shot a teamster through the heart, simply because the man talked back to him. That the man was shot through the heart is beyond doubt, but aside from that all is hearsay. The narrator does not say he even saw Slade on that occasion; and if the homicide occurred in 1860, someone other than Slade was the wagon-boss, for Slade was then hundreds of miles to the eastward attending to his duties as a division-agent along the Overland. He was not engaged in freighting until two years after 1860—after his employment with the Overland had ceased.

At intervals, which grew more widely separated, he found it necessary to make an example of those committing depredations along the line of the stage road. It is related that at one time, while a number of emigrants were proceeding along the road, some of their stock suddenly disappeared. Being apprised of the facts, Slade, with another man, made his way to a ranch where he thought, because of the character of the occupants, the stock probably had been taken. Finding his suspicions verified, he and his companions opened the door of the ranch house and commenced blazing away at the thieves, three of whom were killed and a fourth badly wounded. Probably the story was exaggerated.

Before he had finished his conquest upon the Rocky Ridge Division, one Jules Savoie, a saloon keeper, was indiscreet enough to imbibe his own poison and, while under the influence, boasted in the presence of two of Slade's drivers that he proposed to shoot Slade; he predicted that, when he once got after Slade, there wouldn't be found a horse strong or fast enough to carry Slade beyond the reach of his vengeance.

Slade, hearing of this incipient rebellion within his domain, indiscreetly told two of his men to "go down and clean out old Savoie." Eager to carry out the orders of their superior, the men went down to the Savoie saloon, imbibed deeply, precipitated a fight with Savoie and during the melee killed him and his squaw and burned the house over them. One of the children, a girl, fled into the brush nearby and froze to death. A boy, belonging to the couple, was not harmed. As usual the report, believed by many, was that Slade did the killing himself. The fact seems to be that Slade was greatly disturbed over the occurrence. He had not intended any such dire consequences as the death of Savoie. To make such amends as he could, he and Mrs. Slade thereafter cared for the boy in their home, becoming much attached to him. The youngster was a bright and likeable lad, known as Jemmy Slade.

As illustrative of how Slade constituted himself judge and executioner, a story, well authenticated in the main, comes down to us. In the summer of 1860 there lived upon the Sweetwater, not far from Independence Rock, a Dr. Bartholomew, who had a wife and two small children, a boy of eight and a girl of five. Living not far distant were Charley Bacon and Harry Smith, disreputable and dangerous men. How the trouble arose cannot be definitely ascertained, but Bartholomew came to his death at their hands. One story is that Bartholomew employed them to build a chimney which would not smoke. They erected the chimney but demanded more pay than they had agreed to receive, and, when Bartholomew objected to their exorbitant demands, they shot him. Smith told the widow that he could give her a good home, and, when she scorned his proposition, he ordered her to "hit the road." She was advised to tell her story to the mighty Slade.

Four miles above where Bacon and Smith lived, resided Joseph Plante, a wealthy French Canadian, who maintained a good-sized store; and he had the favor of Slade. Shortly after the killing of Bartholomew, Bacon and Smith planned to kill Plante and take possession of his property. Plante, having discovered the scheme, wrote to Slade about it and also reported the killing of Bartholomew. Slade on Tuesday wrote Plante telling him to sit in his store with a shotgun loaded with buckshot until he came. "I will be there next Friday and I will fix those fellows. Have two lariats ready."

On Friday Slade with four men arrived in an extra coach. The villains were found at Bartholomew's playing cards with a man named Pete. Slade commanded the card-players to throw up their hands, which they did promptly; then he ordered Plante and his drivers to hang them. Some say all three took part in the killing of Bartholomew. However that may be, the executioners undoubtedly did not make any mistake in hanging Pete, who was a blood-thirsty outlaw. Plante, it seems, thought Smith and Pete had killed Bartholomew and proceeded with their execution. When Plante and the drivers were about to hang Pete and Smith, one of them said, "You wouldn't hang a man without giving him a drink of whiskey, would you?" The whiskey was given the two and, when about to drink it, one gave this toast, "May we meet in Hell in half an hour." They were speeded to the meeting. Slade then said, "Plante, you have done the best day's work you ever did in your life, but why did you let Bacon get away? He is the worst of the three." "All right," said Plante, "we'll hang him, too." And they did.

Slade took from the persons of the murderers $523 in cash, and then with Plante set out to call upon Mrs. Bartholomew, for the purpose of ascertaining what course she desired to follow. He urged her to stay upon the ranch, saying she could hire someone to care for the cattle and horses, and with the equipment she possessed she could make a good living for herself and children. She said no, she could not do it, she preferred to go to her father and mother in Omaha. Slade took Mrs. Bartholomew and children to his home, where they were cared for during the ensuing month. Mrs. Slade from her old clothes made enough clothes to last the children for a year and gave to Mrs. Bartholomew a number of dresses. The two women were nearly of a size.

Going back to the Bartholomew ranch, Slade decided to sell it and the livestock to an employee of Plante. The man had a thousand dollars in gold; Plante helped out the sale by guaranteeing the full purchase price. Slade gave Mrs. Bartholomew the money received from the sale of the ranch and livestock and that taken from the outlaws and furnished her and the children a pass to the Missouri River. The widow and children arrived at their destination safely. Mrs. Bartholomew kept up a regular correspondence with the Slades until they moved way from Virginia Dale. News of the hanging, losing nothing in the telling, went up and down the line, but no word of the kindness of the Slades to the widow and children went out along the Overland. Perhaps the Slades kept silent respecting their charities. Some people do.

In passing, it seems that Bacon located his ranch as early as 1857 and took in Smith as a partner in 1859. Prior to that Plante had located his place at what was called the crossing of the Lone Rock River, this being the Indian name for the stream because of the lone rock which was located upon its bank which the white people called Independence Rock. Plante came there to build a bridge across the river. Before the bridge was completed, a freight train attempted to ford the stream, which was high at the time. A wagon loaded with sugar crossed over last. The sand at the bottom of the river had been pretty well cut up and the water was quite deep, at least three feet, with a swift current. Those in charge of the train had raised the wagon box on blocks to keep the sugar from getting wet. When the wagon got into the middle of the stream, the mules could pull it no further. While the teamsters were preparing to put on another team, the water washed the sand from under the lower wheels faster than from the upper ones. The wagon commenced to tip and soon over it went. The teamsters carried such sugar as they could to the bank of the river and laid it upon the grass. Plante bought the sugar. When dry it was hard as a board, but when chopped into lumps it was a favorite article with the Indians who came to Plante's to trade. This legend was what gave the stream the name Sweetwater.

The year 1862 brought to an end Slade's service with the Overland. It seems that 1861 had brought to a close any resistance to his authority. Murderers and thieves chose to behave themselves while within his territory. For a short time he lived quietly and happily with his wife at Virginia Dale. But he missed the excitement of the dangerous days so shortly gone, and could not be satisfied by simply attending to the routine duties of a division-agent. On his trips of inspection, when the stage would stop for a change of horses, he would frequently invite the passengers to drink with him and, while the libations were being prepared, would enliven his guests with stories.

There is general agreement that he was a fascinating story-teller and, when normal, an engaging companion. There seems to be substantial agreement among reliable historians that ever after his designation as superintendent of the Julesburg Division, his sole objective was fidelity to the Overland Stage Company. On occasion he would go upon a spree even when he was agent at Kearney. He would go to Atchison, Kansas, for a short high time; and, when matters seemed to be running along satisfactorily during his latter service, he would take short periods off during which, no doubt, he indulged in liquor, a dangerous practice for him with his peculiar temperament. But during all the forepart of his service, these lapses did not seem noteworthy to his superiors. It cannot be doubted that from the beginning until the end of his employment by the Overland his service to the company and the traveling public was beneficial to a high degree. Indeed, the authors of *The Overland Stage to California* say, despite some malevolent criticism based on hearsay:

He [Slade] was a sort of vigilance committee single-handed, and it was through his efforts that the line was eventually cleared of one of the worst gangs that ever held forth on the plains. Jules and his crowd having been effectually disposed of, and matters elsewhere having been attended to by Ficklin's orders, the line was shortly put in perfect order, and from that time on the stages ran with great regularity. . . . While in the employ of the stage company he was faithful to the trusts imposed on him.

This must have been based on general reputation because Root did not come into the company employ for over a year. His occasional lapses with indulgence in intoxicating liquor disintegrated into sprees. His visits to Denver became frequent. He purchased a beaded and gaudily colored buckskin suit which cost him $750, with which he adorned himself when he went to that city.

Upon his excursions, always with one or two companions, he created a disturbance. His reputation as a killer was well known and he was feared. Upon occasions he would flourish his revolver and discharge it, and he continually exhibited Jules' ears when purchasing liquor. His spree finished, he would return to duty as if nothing had happened. On one spree,

97

shooting carelessly, he seriously wounded one of his best friends. Filled with remorse, he hung abut the hospital until he was assured that his friend would recover and did his utmost to bring him back to health.

His superiors were not much concerned with his antics in Denver or other places, so long as he did not permit his absences to interfere with his duties. Even when a Denver newspaper severely criticized Slade's actions editorially, it is said that Ben Holladay himself called upon the editor and took him to task for his aspersions upon his favorite division-agent.

But Slade's disposition became more and more bent on the destruction of property. He delighted in riding into a saloon or store and wrecking the place. Upon regaining sobriety, he would call upon the proprietor of the demolished place of business and make financial amends. Finally he entered upon a spree at Fort Halleck and, following his propensity of destroying property, wrecked the store of the sutler. This was too much. The army authorities complained to Slade's superiors and insisted that he should be discharged. In view of existing conditions the friendship of the army was so essential there was no denying the request: it amounted to an order.

That Holladay, Ficklin, and the rest were loath to part with the services of their potent superintendent is not to be wondered at. He had executive ability of the highest order and his fidelity to his trust was never doubted.

Langford says: No more exalted tribute can be paid to his character than to say that he organized, managed and controlled for several years, acceptably to the public and the company, and to the employees of the company, the great central division of the Overland stage route through six hundred miles of territory destitute of inhabitants and law, exposed for the entire distance to hostile Indians and overrun with a wild, reckless class of freebooters who maintained

their infamous assumptions with pistol and bowie knife. No man
without a peculiar fitness for such a position could have done this.

That while he was in control of his difficult divisions he was
responsible for actions outside the law, and that they were
carried out under circumstances of terror, there can be no
question. Unless one considers the surrounding circumstances,
the savage characters with which he had to deal, and carries in
mind the realization that he was subject at all times to instant
death at the hands of murderers and thieves who infested a
lawless region hundreds of miles from civilization, Slade's actions seem unpardonable. Probably no man in American history has been so misrepresented. His name became a synonym
for all that is infamous and cruel in human character.

And yet Langford concludes, after a careful examination
shortly after the death of Slade and while the facts were well
known to hundreds of men then living, "Not one of all the
great number of men in control or of those associated with
him as employees of the Overland Stage Company, men personally cognizant of his career, believes that he committed a
single act not justified by the circumstances provoking it."

Demoted from his position of great authority, Slade turned
to his old and profitable occupation of freighting. He could
not realize that his power was gone. He still carried Jules's
ears. He had been used to dominating every situation with
which he was confronted and he could not become used to
occupying a different role.

It was in June of 1863 that he had the encounter with James
Williams over the leadership of the wagon train. When Wil-
liams was elected and said of Slade afterwards, "I appointed
Slade my lieutenant and I never had a man work with me that
I got along with better," it is consistent with the testimony

of others. It was said that this was one of Slade's peculiarities, that if he was "ever put down by a man, which was not often, he always seemed to remember it and was civil to him afterwards."

In the spring or early summer of 1863, Slade visited his old home at Carlyle, Illinois. So far as we are informed, nothing was said to him of the unfortunate occurrence which caused him to leave his home so many years before. Returning to Virginia Dale, he learned of the fabulous gold discoveries upon Grasshopper and Alder Gulches, at that time part of Idaho and afterwards a part of Montana; and he concluded to seek that new and promising region. Learning that Henry S. Gilbert, who had been a station-agent upon the Overland, was leaving for Alder Gulch with his family shortly, Slade conferred with him, evidently with the idea of transporting a portion of Gilbert's household goods. This was arranged, and Slade was also to take with him some of Gilbert's cattle and a number of horses.

One might suppose from the reputation some had given Slade that Gilbert would hesitate to entrust him with practically all his worldly goods. No such thing. Gilbert, a level-headed man, and for many years an outstanding citizen of Virginia City, knew the facts, and knew that no man along the Overland bore or deserved a higher reputation for honesty and fidelity to his trust than did that famous man. Mr. Gilbert arrived at his destination on September 1, 1863, and Slade arrived less than a month later. Gilbert warned Slade that he could not safely destroy property, drunk or sober, as he had been doing on occasion, that the class of men with whom he had now cast his lot would not tolerate any such conduct. This was reiterated to Slade after his first drunken outbreak in Virginia City, during which he had been guilty of misconduct.

Slade answered that he did not intend to kill anyone and that he would pay for whatever damage he did.

Slade had not been long in the new mining camp when he had an opportunity to make use of his freighting outfit. A steamboat, loaded with general merchandise, had left St. Joseph, Missouri, too late in the summer to reach Fort Benton. The cargo was unloaded at the mouth of Milk River. J. B. Hardie, one of the owners of the merchandise, came to Virginia City to arrange for transporting the merchandise thither. Slade undertook the transportation. There was no wagon road over a large part of the hundreds of miles between Virginia City and Milk River. Nevertheless, Slade, with his extraordinary faculty of getting things done, made his way to the mouth of Milk River, traversing country over which wagon wheel had never rolled before, and accomplished the seemingly impossible feat of returning with his loaded wagons to Virginia City by the first of November.[4] By this accomplishment he made for himself a large sum of money.

Winter having closed in, making profitable freighting impractical, he went over the Tobacco Root mountain range, which separates Alder Gulch from the Madison Valley, and located a ranch on the banks of the Madison a little southerly from the mouth of Meadow Creek, to which he gave the name "Ravenswood." Is it not worthy of remark that a man bearing

---

[4] In the early nineties I went from White Sulphur Springs to the vicinity of Martinsdale. Sitting with the stage-driver, I saw on the right of the road on which we were traveling a cut or notch almost straight down a long hillside. Asking the driver what caused it, he said "that man Slade had to rough lock his wheels to get off that high bench when he was on his way to the mouth of Milk River to get freight the streamboat had unloaded on the south side of the Missouri. He must have got back some different way." About thirty years had passed since Slade had made the journey. L.L.C.

the character attributed generally to Slade along the Overland would have chosen such a name?

Ranching was not a sufficient outlet for his energies. One way then traveled in going from Virginia City to the Gallatin Valley passed over the Tobacco Root Range, a rough trail up the mountainside and then down to the Madison Valley through a canyon in the bottom of which ran a boisterous little stream, to be known as Slade Creek. He conceived the idea of building along the course of the trail a passable road to serve the traveling public, charging toll for its use. To this task he set himself, first building a stone house at the point where he purposed to set up his toll-gate. This house was more comfortable than the bleak one on the windy point at Ravenswood, and here he and Mrs. Slade settled down for the winter. The pine trees along the mountain slope provided ample firewood, and it may be supposed that the couple looked forward to the most peaceful period in their married life. It was too quiet for Slade.

He made frequent trips to Virginia City, despite the protests of his wife, and upon each occasion fell in with convivial companions who found him delightful. One of his chief cronies was William H. Fairweather, leader of the "Discovery Party"—the party which made the discovery of gold in Alder Creek—and a man whom everybody liked. These two, and some others, would enliven the night with their celebrations. In paying for the drinks, Jules's ears invariably came into play. The people had heard Slade would do this but doubted the truth of the story. They were shocked when they observed the gruesome relics. Notwithstanding the fact that the Vigilantes were then engaged in their salutary work and Slade had been warned that he must cease from making trouble, at the end of a spree he would mount his horse, ride up and down the streets firing his revolver, and occasionally would ride into a

ade's stone house, seven miles from Virginia City, Montana. Mrs. Slade made her sperate ride from here to try to save her husband's life. Courtesy of Montana Historical ciety.

saloon and wreck the place. He would then return to the toll house and shortly would ride into Virginia City and pay for all the damage he had committed. Nor did he confine his drunken activities to Virginia City. He frequently rode down the gulch, stopping in the towns of Central, Nevada, Adobetown, and Junction, where he patronized the saloons, and occasionally wrecked one.

Once in a while he would ride his horse into a store. But he never attempted to ride into the store kept by the Lott brothers, John S. and Mortimer H. They had told him that to do so was highly dangerous. He took their word. He knew, too, that

John S. Lott had led the Vigilante expedition to Bannack where Henry Plummer, miners' sheriff and at the same time road-agent chief, and his principal deputies Stinson and Ray, were hanged on January 10, 1864.

During January and February, 1864, the Vigilantes had hanged the principal members of Henry Plummer's road-agent band and had banished many others. After the execution of the five in Virginia City on January 14th, Alder Gulch was quiet. The people were safe in their lives and property. But in February Slade made several visits to Virginia City and was guilty of serious breaches of the peace. About the first of March he so terrified the inhabitants that some of the store keepers locked their doors. Not only that but when he ran out of money the ears of Jules were offered, and at the point of the gun the saloonkeeper agreed these gruesome objects were legal tender. On this expedition he did considerable damage for which he was unable to pay. About a week later he came to the city and entered upon a protracted and his last drinking bout. During this orgy he and a companion entered a theater where by boisterous conduct and rough speech they insulted not only the actresses but the people in the audience. Indignation against Slade and his companion ran high, and the offenders were ejected from the theater. Later in the evening Slade terrorized a portion of the city. He and his companions disturbed the night by singing a ribald song in which certain leading citizens were referred to in no complimentary terms. A silly story is that this played a part in that which befell Slade. The high-minded and distinguished men upon whose memory the imputation was cast were above any such puerile thought.

March 9, 1864, dawned. Slade was still intoxicated—he had been up all night—but seemingly not ill-natured. He was in a prankish mood. Seeing a milk wagon coming up the street he beckoned the driver to drive to the door of the saloon in front of which Slade and his tipsy comrades were assembled. When the driver stopped, Slade said he was thirsty and he desired some milk, he wanted a gallon! He was thirsty! When the milk man gave him a gallon can, Slade, who had bestrode the wagon wheel and was having difficulty in maintaining his balance, attempted to drink but spilled the milk upon his shirt front. When his companions laughed, Slade emptied the rest of the milk over the milkman's head. When his companions laughed louder, Slade chortled in glee.

His good humor continued until he was served with a warrant of arrest. Slade, with his companions, at the request of miners' sheriff Fox, went to the court room where Fox attempted to read the warrant. Instead of submitting quietly as he had done on two or three previous occasions, Slade became enraged, seized the warrant, tore it in pieces, threw the fragments upon the floor, and spat upon them. At the same time the clicking of the revolvers of his companions warned the sheriff to proceed no further, and with good judgment he appeared to consider the incident closed. Not satisfied with that, Slade immediately sought out Alexander Davis, the miners' judge, who had issued the warrant, and said to him, "I understand you have placed me under a thousand dollar bail." Taking from his pocket a 41 calibre Derringer he placed the point of the barrel against the judge's forehead and said, "You are my bail," then left and began to resume his drinking, the ears of Jules again serving as legal tender. He had degenerated into a hell-raiser when drinking, ruthless and defiant, but he, in all the time since his arrival at Virginia City, had not committed any offense ranking above a mere misdemeanor.

Matters had now reached a serious pass. The Vigilantes had observed what was transpiring and there was considerable ominous talk. One of the foremost members of that organization met Slade and said to him, "Slade, you get your horse at once and go home, or there will be hell to pay." Slade appeared startled and inquired, "What do you mean?" But the Vigilante quietly and with deep earnestness said, "You have no right to ask me what I mean; get your horse at once and remember what I tell you." Slade promised to do so and mounted his horse. Then he temporized. Never did man tempt fate more recklessly. He began again to ride the streets. The storekeepers closed their places of business. As he rode Slade berated two leading members of the Vigilantes, coupling their names with that of a woman who was not unknown to fame. The warning given by his Vigilante friend was unheeded. He had said that he was himself a Vigilante, but apparently he thought that the sole function of the organization was to punish thieves and murderers in accordance with their public announcement. During this day Captain Williams, executive officer of the Vigilantes, a patient man, asked Alexander Toponce[5] to tell Slade he had better go home. Toponce did so, and Slade got on his horse, but dismounted to have just one more drink. The night passed. Apparently he had concluded to go home and mounted his horse again. Seeing two or three well known Vigilantes, he said, "I guess the Vigilantes are played out." One of them, X. Beidler, replied: "You will find out whether or not they are played out within three hours."

Those of the executive committee in Virginia City thought it time to act. They sent a messenger to Captain Williams, who lived at Nevada City, advising him of the situation. Williams called to his aid John S. Lott, treasurer of the committee and his right-hand man, and the two assembled two hundred armed miners, who quickly marched the intervening mile be-

[5] Alexander Toponce, *Reminiscences of Alexander Toponce* (Ogden, Utah: Mrs. Kate Toponce, 1923; reprint ed., Norman: University of Oklahoma Press, 1971).

tween Nevada City and Virginia City. In the meantime Slade heard that Williams had been appealed to. Sensing serious trouble, he went to the store of Pfouts & Russell and apologized abjectly to Mr. Pfouts, president of the Vigilantes. He was too late. As he talked with Pfouts, Williams and Lott entered. Characteristically, Williams did not waste any words. He said: "Slade, I want you." "What do you want with me?" "Come along and ask no questions." Pale as a ghost, Slade submitted quietly and went with his captors.

The entire executive committee went into session. Some were Slade's friends. All were reluctant to administer the extreme punishment and decided to put the matter to the assembly. After deliberation the assembly decided that Slade's execution was imperative. While the committee was deliberating, a friend of Slade's, seeing the gravity of the situation, went at the top speed of his horse to warn Mrs. Slade of what was impending. She did not waste a moment. Almost distracted with love and fear, she saddled her well-known fast horse and set out to rescue once again the object of her undivided devotion. With all the skill of a perfect equestrienne she urged the great horse up the heavy grade to the mountain top. From there she could see the city two miles below. Could she arrive in time? The road was steep and rocky, dangerous at high speed. But she did not hestitate. Down the declivity she plunged regardless of danger to herself or horse, risking the loss of all if she should fall. The crowd saw her coming at breakneck speed, her raven tresses blown by the strong March wind. It was a thrilling sight.

Virginia City lies on either side of Daylight Creek. Below the site of the stone building of Pfouts & Russell the valley widened into a flat in which was located an auction corral. At the eastern gate there were posts strong and high, with a heavy beam running from one to the other. A rope with the seven-looped knot was suspended from the beam and, underneath, a dry goods box was placed. To this place was brought Slade. Instantly sobered by the decision of the Vigilantes, he was completely unnerved. Let no man say he was a coward. Stunned at first by the dreadful sentence, he pleaded for his life with the eloquence of despair. But his awful record—his reputation as a killer, the ears of Jules in his pocket—overcame his piteous appeals. When he thought of his wife he grew frantic—"O, my dear wife!"

Many of his friends, powerless to interfere, wept bitterly. One, finding his entreaties futile, threw off his coat, declaring that Slade could be executed only over his dead body. A hundred guns changed his mind. He attempted to escape, was brought back, resumed his coat, and promised to be good. Leading men of the community appealed to by the condemned, men who liked and pitied him, answered that they could do nothing. It became known that Mrs. Slade was coming. She had frequently attended the social gatherings, participated in the dances, in Alder Gulch. She was admired and popular.

The committee well understood that Mrs. Slade would not hesitate to attempt a rescue force and there is little doubt that she would have been supported by armed men who not only were friends of Slade but who resented what they deemed the unauthorized—some said the outrageous—action of the Vigilante Committee. The leaders had determined that the execution of Slade was necessary if there was not to be a return to lawlessness in Alder Gulch. Her arrival before the execution probably would mean bloodshed. There was no escape from duty now, the execution must go on. Williams, not given to vacillation, gave the well-known and final order, "Men, do your duty."

So the mighty Slade, the ears of Jules in his pocket, departed. Such, says Dimsdale, was Captain J. A. Slade, "the idol of his followers, the terror of his enemies and of all that were not within the charmed circle of his dependents. In him, generosity and destructiveness, brutal lawlessness and courteous kindness, firm friendship and volcanic outbreaks of fury, were so mingled that he seems like one born out of date. He should have lived in feudal times, and have been the comrade of the Front de Boeuff, De Lacys, and Bois Guilberts, of days almost forgotten."

Save for this execution, the Vigilantes of Montana have been well-nigh universally commended. For this act they have been fiercely condemned and as vigorously commended.

The exigency seemed great. Was there to be regularity of human conduct in those mountains? Was law and order, so recently established in a vast region where there was no organized government, to cease, and was all that which had been gained to be lost? It must not be forgotten that the Vigilantes were patriots whose only purpose was to make their world a save place for honest men. Dimsdale summed it up: "The death of Slade was the protest of society on behalf of social order and the rights of man."

When Slade was pronounced dead, his body was taken at once to the Virginia Hotel, where it was placed in the best room, awaiting the arrival of Mrs. Slade. Her demonstrations over her dead husband left no doubt of the sincerity of her devotion to him. Her paroxysms of grief were so intense that she was unable to compose herself for hours. She reproached her friends bitterly. Why did not they, the friends of Slade, shoot him to prevent his death upon the scaffold? She would have done it. "No dog's death should have come to such a man!"

An interesting sidelight on this is that many years later when the pioneers met in Virginia City in 1898, Charles W. Cannon, a prominent citizen of Helena, came to the great meeting. As you will surmise, the memories of the old timers were awakened and there was much reminiscence.

Mr. Cannon told a small group, of which I was one, of his harrowing personal experience which happened after the execution of the famous Joseph Alfred Slade by the Vigilantes:

I knew Slade and his wife well, [said Mr. Cannon]. Mrs. Slade was a tall, brilliant woman, probably the best dancer in town. She then was a good woman, a general favorite; but she became a tigress after Slade was hanged. Somehow she got the idea that I was a Vigilante and was active in carrying out the sentence on her husband. She threatened to kill me and several others on sight. A few days after the hanging I was in the store in which I worked.

I suppose you know how we had to carry on in those long, narrow, log buildings. In this clothing store we had tables end to end down the center, upon which we piled all sorts of clothes, coats, pants, shirts, and the like.

Some fellow came running into the store yelling "Charlie look out! Mrs. Slade is coming!" Just as she came in the front door flourishing one of those big powder and ball six shooters . . . I dived under one of the tables . . . near the back door. She did not see me. She went up and down the aisles of the store swearing she would kill me, but as she was unable to find me, she went away. In the meantime I had escaped.

The next day I had to go to Salt Lake on business for the firm. I was so busy I neglected to arrange for a seat on the stage.[6] I got to the coach in time, but there were two fellows sitting with the driver, so I had to crawl inside. All the seats were taken except one in the middle. I took it and the coach started. I looked around and to my horror Mrs. Slade was in the back seat directly behind me.

The stage didn't stop for twenty miles. Mrs. Slade had on that six-shooter, and I did not know when she might shoot me. When we

[6]See Appendix C for an account of travel by stage in this era.

stopped to change horses I got out and gave one of the passengers who had been sitting with the driver twenty dollars for his seat. As I look back I suppose I wasn't in any danger that day, but certainly I wasn't comfortable. Mrs. Slade got over her animosity after a while. In fact, early next year she married Jim Kiskadden, and he was a Vigilante.

Mrs. Slade had not let Slade rest among his enemies, however. A zinc coffin was procured in which Slade's remains were preserved in alcohol. This receptacle was incased in a box which was taken over the mountain and buried across the road from the rock house, where the grave was within her view. She remained there until July, grief stricken, disconsolate, and revengeful. Then she transferred the body of Joseph Alfred Slade to Salt Lake, where it was interred in the old Mormon cemetery, July 20, 1864, to remain there until she could convey it to the burial place of his father at Clinton, Illinois. But that purpose was not to be fulfilled. The body remains in one of the most beautiful spots of the cemetery in Salt Lake, but the identity of the grave is lost. Like much of Slade's history, obscurity shadows his resting place.

While the Vigilantes started out with the policy that the only punishment which the organization would inflict should be death, that policy was changed by necessity. There were many men whom they believed deserving of death, but they were unable to procure irrefutable evidence of guilt. The Vigilantes were not satisfied with proving a man guilty beyond a reasonable doubt; they required what amounted to absolute certainty. They, therefore, decreed banishment for many of the roughs who they felt deserved the extreme penalty, and, in doing so, they sometimes erred, for those who were banished continued their practices of robbery and murder.

Another modification respecting punishment was made

when the committee found it necessary to check the commission of lesser crimes, and whipping the malefactor was resorted to.

After the execution of Slade, it looked for a period as if the Vigilantes' work was done. They soon discovered their error.

CHAPTER SIX

The Meaning of 3–7–77

Capture, trial, and hanging of Kelly. Long arm of the Vigilantes reaches Dolan. Vigilantes organized in Last Chance Gulch (Helena). John X. Beidler the leader. Speculation on the meaning of 3-7-77.

IN THE SUMMER OF 1864 they were called upon to prove to the "roughs" still in the gulch that the organization had not disbanded. Two men, James Brady and Jim Kelly, at Nevada City, attempted to assassinate another by shooting through the window into the room in which the victim was. The man was hurt, seriously but not fatally. Williams heard the shots just as he was going to bed, but noise of that sort was common; he paid no special attention to it. He was summoned by a friend, who told him a man had been shot. Kelly was arrested immediately, Brady after some difficulty, as he had fled. Brady was identified by his victim and, as the death of the wounded man was hourly expected, was placed upon trial as for murder, during which he confessed that he had fired the shot. The committee pronounced the death sentence. There was not sufficient evidence against Kelly to warrant the infliction of the death penalty, but the committee determined to punish him severely; and he was sentenced to receive 50 lashes on his bare back.

At four o'clock in the afternoon, Brady was taken from his place of confinement to the gallows, under the escort of 200 armed men. Standing beneath the gallows, Brady addressed the crowd, attempting to excuse himself for his act by saying that he was intoxicated and insane but he hoped his execution would be a warning to others.

After the execution, the sentence upon Kelly was duly carried out, and he was ordered to leave the country. It was a mistake to let this Kelly go. It appeared later that in the month of July, 1864, he had been involved in the robbery of a coach going from Virginia City to Salt Lake. After investigation, Williams with 21 veteran Vigilantes left Nevada on August 28th, camping at the Williams ranch for the night, and, after a hard ride extending over a number of days, reached Meek and Gibbon's ferry on Snake River. There it was learned that Kelly had been continuing his career of outlawry after leaving Alder Gulch. Informed that Kelly, in the course of his thieving, had gone toward Portneuf Canyon, the captain with a posse, ten in all, rode there, making a night march, "camping at 11 o'clock without feed for man or beast during a hurricane of wind." At two o'clock in the morning they were in the saddle again, traveling until daybreak, when they saw a camp fire. They were hungry and went directly thereto, having visions of breakfast, but found it was a Shoshone Indian camp and the Indians had little but chokecherries to eat.

The Indian chief, however, offered Captain Williams a broiled trout, which he ate and then fell asleep, while the others ate chokecherries supplied by the papooses. Seeing the captain asleep when the sun arose, an old squaw considerately built a low willow wigwam over him, and, when he awoke, he was visibly astonished and bewildered at what he deemed his prison house, to the amusement of the Indians and the members of his command, who laughed heartily over his seeming predicament.

The posse started on, reaching Portneuf at 11 in the morning, learning during the breakfast hour that a party of California prospectors had caught Kelly in a haystack some distance from Portneuf station. On their way to join the Californians, Williams, who was riding ahead, saw the dead body of a man floating in the creek. It was found that the man had been shot in the back of the head, his body wrapped in a gray blanket, and then thrown into the stream. Two nearby camp fires seemed to be 10 or 15 days old. During the recovery and burial of the body, Williams said, "Boys, I have a feeling that I will be present at the execution of the murderer of this man within a year."

Kelly was found in the custody of the Californians. A trial was called immediately, and, upon the evidence adduced, Kelly was condemned to death. He said he thought it was pretty rough to hang him after he had submitted to the whipping in Alder Gulch, but called for a smoke, which he enjoyed. In his presence the hangman's knot was tied and the party marched to a tree where preparations for the execution were completed. Here occurred another amusing incident of the trip—amusing to the Vigilantes, perhaps, because it somewhat relieved the tension necessarily attendant upon the infliction of the terrible penalty.

At the very spot of execution there was an Indian camp and the warriors were lying about well-nigh surfeited after a hot dog (not hotdog) dinner. Some seem to think the Indian's stomach is not affected by the condition of his nerves, but, as this happening tends to show, that idea is erroneous. The Indian has a horror of death by hanging; the warriors viewed the gruesome, business-like preparations with amazement, then consternation, and, when the body of the condemned man was launched into the air, the warriors lost their dinners. The Californians arrived about this time and assisted the Vigilantes by burying the outlaw in a willow coffin which they constructed. The Vigilantes then returned home.

Shortly thereafter they found that a man named John Dolan had robbed one Brady, a resident of Nevada, of $700 in gold and had fled the country. The identity of the robber was not known for some time, but, when it was ascertained that Dolan was the man, the executive committee dispatched a Vigilante—probably Thomas Baume—to Salt Lake City with directions to arrest him and bring him to Alder Gulch. The arm of the Vigilantes was long.

In the meantime it was discovered that Dolan was an associate of Kelley, but recently hanged at Snake River. When the Vigilante got back to Alder Gulch with his captive, Dolan was placed on trial. Stolen nuggets worth $300 were in his possession when he was arrested. After a lengthy trial Dolan was found guilty, and sentenced to death by unanimous vote. He then broke down, confessed the crime, and offered to make up the balance, $400, if he were let go. To this the committee refused to accede. The execution was attended by an unusual show of force; companies of Vigilantes from Highland, Pine Grove, and Virginia City having joined the companies already on the ground from Nevada and Junction. When all was ready, Captain Williams addressed the crowd stating, according to Dimsdale, that the execution of criminals such as Dolan was a matter of public necessity in a mining country and that the safety of the community from outlawry and outrage was the only reason that dictated it.

He finished by saying in a manner that all understood, "It has been said that you will rescue the prisoner; don't try it, for fear of the consequences. What is to be done has been deliberately weighed and determined, and nothing shall prevent the execution of the malefactor."

It is especially noteworthy to record here the fact that by reason of their refusal to permit Dolan to make good the balance to Brady, the man injured by the theft, after the execution the Committee itself paid to Brady the deficiency.

John X. Beidler, the zealous and efficient, had gone to the new mining camp in Last Chance Gulch at Helena, and it is probable that he organized a branch of the Vigilantes there. At any rate he appears to have been the leading spirit in maintaining law and order in Last Chance. He superintended the execution of Keene and other outlaws at Helena. That he was acting in conjunction with the Vigilance Committee at Virginia City is pretty evident.

Shortly after the discovery of gold in Confederate Gulch it was reported to Beidler that robberies were being perpetrated at Diamond City and that a villainous looking character was strongly suspected of the crimes; he had been arrested, charged with robbery, obtaining goods under false pretenses, and the like. This information having been conveyed to Virginia City, the committee concluded to take a hand, and Captain Williams rode to Helena at once; upon his arrival a captain with four or five men was dispatched to Diamond City with orders to bring the prisoner to Helena; they departed at once.

On the next day Williams and Beidler met the party and accompanied it with the prisoner to the city. The prisoner, who had been going under the name of Jack Silvie, but whose name probably was Jacob Seachriest, was confined in a cabin, the same one in which John Keene had been incarcerated; and a strong guard was placed about it.

The Committee heard the evidence produced, together with a statement of the prisoner in which they found many important contradictions. The members consulted, but were

John X. Beidler, famous member of the Vigilantes. Courtesy of Montana Historical Society.

unable to satisfy themselves upon the matter. The prisoner was given another examination, and a thorough cross-examination—cross-examination is often "the sword of truth"—as a result of which the committee was satisfied that he was a desperado and deserved death. He finally made a full confession and there are two accounts as to how it was brought about. One is that the Vigilantes invited (commanded) a minister of the gospel to join the prisoner in the cabin and pray with him for the purpose of wringing a confession from him, and that the minister, after having labored fervently with the wretch, finally broke down his reserve and obtained a full confession.

That through the minister's efforts the prisoner prayed to his Maker for forgiveness, there is not much doubt. The other story is that the confession did not come until the culprit was under the hangman's tree in Dry Gulch. Whenever it was, during the confession the prisoner stated that he had been engaged in robbery and murder for a dozen years, his last murder having been that committed on the Snake River. He had shot his victim, who was sitting by a camp fire, in the back of the head, after which he robbed his victim of all he possessed, wrapped the body in a blanket, and threw it in the creek. Thus it was that the presentiment of Captain Williams that he would be present at the execution of the dead man's murderer within one year was verified.

So far as I know, this was the last action of James Williams as executive officer of the Vigilantes.

He quit his gruesome work with a sigh of great relief and retired as quietly as he could; his departure from his powerful position was even more unostentatious than was his advent into it; thereafter he seldom talked of his connection with the organization, except to those who served with him, and not often with them. He always maintained the closest friendship

A hanging in Helena. Courtesy of Montana Historical Society.

and affection for those who had been associated with him in the work. When he was induced to talk of the actions of the Vigilance Committee, he was generous in his praise of his associates, notably John S. Lott, Neil Howie, X. Beidler, Adriel B. Davis, and others.

Nothing has been said by the historians respecting the activities of a subcommittee of the executive committee, which was called the Ferreting Committee. This was composed of the executive officer and, it would seem, such persons as he detailed from time to time to assist in what might be termed detective and other executive work.

From the treasurer's book kept by John S. Lott, it is ascertained that the businessmen and miners of Alder Gulch contributed various amounts aggregating in excess of $3,000 to the "Ferreting Fund." The subscriptions were all made during the year 1864, and most, if not all, of the money was paid out during that year. The first subscription was by Lott & Brother, $25.

Evidently some of the leading Vigilantes canvassed portions of the gulch for subscriptions, as is shown by entries in the treasurer's book. On January 31st, Elk Morse turned in $290.75; Miller paid in $131.95 from the Highland District; Sanders at one time paid in $150 on account of subscriptions. We find the entry, "Samuel Schwab $93.27." David paid in $118.50, probably from Junction. The subscription work seems to have continued throughout the year. On September 17th, Peter Hartwig turned in $102.50 from the Highland District, and Pfouts, the president of the committee, on the same day submitted an order on Baume Angevine & Co. for $1,364.60. On October 5th, the Summit District turned in $225.45, and Nevada City $342.95. A large number of individuals gave sums of money ranging in different amounts from fifty cents up to $50. The Virginia City brewery gave $25; the Gem saloon

$25. Well-known names appear: Allen & Millard, the pioneer bankers; Strasburger & Bro.; Kessler & Co.; O. W. Jay; J. H. Ming; Griffith & Thompson; Poznanski & Co.; Oliver & Co.; Dance & Stuart. "Somebody" gave $25.

The money was paid out generally upon Williams's order, but here and there appears an order given by Clark, probably "Old Man" Clark, Brown—Charley Brown—or Morse. Evidently Brown, Clark, and Morse were members of the Ferreting Committee. Morse at one time gave an order for $5 for rope. A Mexican woman was paid $50 for a pistol. Schwab was paid $110 for a horse, saddle, and bridle. The sum of $3.50 was paid for a pistol damaged by Brown. Sums of money were paid to well-known Vigilantes, for example, to Hereford $20; to David $87.86 for expenses on a "trip to Gallatin," undoubtedly the one which resulted in the execution of Bill Hunter; the fare of Morse to Salt Lake by overland stage cost $75; A. B. Hamilton was reimbursed $42.50 for money expended for the committee, and William Clark $72 for a like account. At one place in the treasurer's book is recorded that the committee at Summit paid $100 for a house in which to hold meetings. Nothing appears to have been paid to any member of the committee for his personal services.

It was all paid out for necessary expense. Davis says that Williams lost six horses and worked with the Vigilance committee for more than a year without one penny of compensation and "did more hard riding than any five men in the whole outfit."

John Lott, writing to me, says, "You will see that Williams was really the executive head, but Pfouts was the ornamental [sic] one, and a good one, too."

So far nothing has been said of 3-7-77, the numerals of Nemesis. Whence this mysterious symbol, what did it mean, and to what extent was it used? Undoubtedly it originated with the Vigilantes of California, who used it during the years when William T. Coleman was the guiding genius of the organization at San Francisco. The Vigilantes of Denver used 3-7-77 and also 3-11-77, as did the Montana Vigilantes. Each set of figures is euphonious, but 3-7-77 is smoother than 3-11-77. The sign was used as a warning and its purpose was to give the person warned a reasonable, if short time, in which to leave the locality—and to keep on going.

Those ministers of retributive justice who were constrained to act in the absence of any legal machinery in Alder Gulch knew their psychology—they understood the power of a dread which dwells in a mystery of lethal import; and the numerals meant that a secret, swift-moving band was warning that the end of life by the hangman's knot was near.

The understanding in Alder Gulch always was that when a man found the sign 3-7-77 on his door or tentflap or wagon, he had 3 hours, 7 minutes, and 77 seconds to leave camp. I have talked with many Vigilantes about this sign and everyone gave that interpretation. "3-11-77 simply gave the man four minutes more," said a Vigilante with a chuckle. Thus the person warned had practically half of a business day to put his affairs in order and start his journey thence. It was a standing joke in the early days that nobody took his full time.

Another joke, current during the 1870's, was that once upon a time a suspicious character arrived at his tent just as a Vigilante had finished writing on the flap in charcoal, "3-7-77." The suspicious character said: "Huh, I've got 3 hours, 7 minutes and 77 seconds to leave camp, have I? If you fellers'll help me ketch my horse, the 77 seconds will be plenty for me; you can have the rest of the time!"

Five or six years ago I was told by a gentleman who was

quite positive about it that 3-7-77 signified the dimensions of a grave—3 feet wide, 7 feet long, and 77 inches deep. I rejoined that if the sign were 3-11-77 the grave would be 3 feet wide, 11 feet long, and 77 inches deep!

Whatever the sign meant in the mind of the man whose invention it was, it meant a warning and one to be obeyed without delay.

The Montana Vigilantes did not begin the use of the symbol before Captain Williams and his avenging company returned from the Bitterroot, probably not until Bill Hunter was executed. It will be remembered that the original endeavor was to capture and execute the miscreants who composed Henry Plummer's road agent band, not to warn them so they might escape. But as has been said, the Vigilantes did not exact the death penalty unless proof of guilt was clear and irrefutable. When it became necessary to rid the country of men who were clearly of the criminal class, but upon whom the committee did not desire to inflict a penalty, the dread warning was used with unfailing efficacy. It is said that the Vigilantes warned the practical jokers, who abounded in Alder Gulch, that the symbol was not to be trifled with and it would be no joke with anyone who sought to joke with it. No jokes were played with that sign!

As we leave the recital of James Williams's activities with the Vigilantes—after the main work of the organization had been completed—it would seem appropriate in making up our judgments upon the character of the work done by that heroic band, which amid so much stress and danger set forth to establish law and order in these mountains, to receive testimony from a high and unprejudiced source. Honorable Hezekiah L. Hosmer, appointed chief justice of Montana, opened the first court in the territory in the dining room of the Planter Hotel in Virginia City on December 5, 1864. In charging the grand jury, the chief justice said:

The assemblage of a Grand Jury in this new territory affords opportunity for a casual survey of the interests committed to its charge. The cause of Justice, hitherto deprived of the intervention of regularly organized courts, has been temporarily subserved by voluntary tribunals of the people partaking more of the nature of self-defense than the comprehensive principles of the common law. It is not part of the business of this court to find fault with what has been done; but rather, in common with all good citizens, to laud the transactions of an organization, which, in the absence of law, assumed the delicate and responsible office of purging society of all offenders against its peace, happiness and safety.

Such societies, originating in necessity, have been communities without law, and in which the penalties of the laws were not proportional to the criminality of the offense. Their adaptation to the necessities of new settlements, has obtained for them an approbation so universal, that they are the first measures resorted to, by well-intentioned men, to free themselves of that vile class of adventurers which infests all unorganized communities for the purpose of fraud, robbery, and murder. In no part of our country have they labored more efficiently than here. No where else did they enter upon their duties, amid greater embarrassments. It was questionable even when they commenced, whether they were numerically equal to the task. The sources of official power have been monopolized by the very class which preyed upon society. The greatest villain of them all—with hands reeking with the blood of numerous victims—was the principal ministerial officer of the territory, and had at his beck a band of wretches who had become hardened in the bloody trade, years before they came here to practice it. In this condition of affairs, there could be but one or two courses to pursue—to hang the offenders or submit to their authority, and give the territory over to misrule and murder. Happily, the former course prevailed, and the

125

summary punishment visited upon a few, frightened the survivors from the territory, and restored order and safety.

His Honor then in vigorous language asserted that the functions of the Vigilantes were no longer necessary and urged all good citizens to join in sustaining the government and its duly constituted officers. He continued:

Let us give to every man, how aggravated soever his crime, the full benefit of the freeman's right—an impartial trial by jury. Vigilantes and courts—and all good men can co-operate in fulfilling the grand purpose of the criminal law; that of bringing offenders to justice, without violating any of its provisions; but the very first element in such a warfare against crime, must be the general recognition of courts of law, as the great conservator of peace and safety.

It is interesting to note that in again charging the grand jury of Madison County a year and a half later, Chief Justice Hosmer said:

The long interval that has elapsed since the last session of the Court in this District affords occasion for a retrospective glance at the condition of judicial affairs, which it may not be unprofitable, at this time, to improve. Little more than one year and a half ago, the first Court of this Territory was organized in this city. Previous to that event the observance of order had been enforced by the efforts of a voluntary association, which originated in necessity, and which had for its object the protection and defense of the people of the Territory against the designs of an organized band of marauders who acknowledge no law, and deemed no crime too great which could accomplish their purposes of robbery and excess. It is no small compliment to the energy and principle of those who formed this association, that they carried their object into effect. The inhabitants of Montana owe much to their fidelity, fortitude, and promptness for, while some of the territories organized anterior to ours are suffering from all the evils of murder, robbery and frequent affrays, ours is as nearly exempted therefrom as any society similarly exposed could expect to be.

Upon Williams's trip to Helena in connection with the Seachriest arrest and execution, he became interested in the new city, then in its early placer boom days, and regarded it as a good place for business. This conclusion probably influenced his course during the succeeding months, for late in 1865 he sold out his interest in the Nevada stable and corral and leased the Western Corral in Helena. There he went, his brother John accompanying him, about the first of June, 1866. In the meantime he had located a homestead on the Ruby, of which mention has heretofore been made. The Helena venture did not prove to the liking of the brothers, and they returned to Alder Gulch in the late fall, the Captain going to the ranch.

CHAPTER SEVEN

Marriage of Captain Williams to Miss Elizabeth Ledford

Prosperity, then misfortune. Hardships of ranch life for women. Captain Williams vs. X. Beidler with practical jokes.

ON JANUARY 9, 1866, the Captain called at the residence of James Ledford and met for the first time Miss Elizabeth Ledford, a native of Audrain County, Missouri, who with her parents had left their home in Missouri on April 10, 1863, and crossed the plains, arriving at Alder Gulch in August, 1863. Miss Ledford was enjoying a birthday party, and the Captain informed her that January 9th was also his natal day.

They jointly celebrated that day each year thereafter, including 1887, for their first meeting was followed by a courtship which ripened into their marriage by Chief Justice Hosmer on December 27, 1866. The couple set up housekeeping at the Captain's ranch immediately, residing there until the fall of 1881, when they moved to the Callaway place some six miles up the river.

The Williams house stood upon the east side of the Salt Lake Road, the barn, sheds, and corrals being on the west side, toward the river. The latchstring was out at all times to their friends, who were numerous; Captain and Mrs. Williams were sociable and nothing pleased them more than receiving callers. Old Vigilante associates of the Captain were especially welcome.

Little ones arrived at the Williams house with great regularity; seven children eventually were playing in their dooryard. From 1866 on, the Captain was engaged in raising livestock, principally cattle. For a long time he prospered, but, in a moment when the outlook appeared brightest, he fell into an irretrievable error. At this period in our early-day history—and it was a somewhat extended period—a practice, well-nigh amounting to a custom, obtained, that of signing promissory notes as an accommodation for one's friends; no one will ever be able to estimate the mischief that followed that practice. Don L. Byam, he who presided as chief judge at the Ives trial, was obliged to borrow a large sum of money from James F. Browne the banker; Theophilus Muffly, son-in-law of Byam, James Williams, and another signed the note as sureties.

It was the old and too familiar story; Judge Byam met with misfortune and was unable to pay. Browne proceeded against the maker of the note and his sureties and took from Williams cattle, horses, and all else he had except that which a beneficent exemption law saved to him and his family. Mrs. Williams never ceased to complain bitterly, but he who had commanded the Vigilantes in parlous times took his medicine without murmur. It was difficult to start again, but by dint of hard work, frugality, and the efforts of a devoted wife, he gradually got upon the upgrade. The hospitality extended to friends was not so lavish as before, but just as hearty.

The life of the ranch woman of that period was hard; at times it was desperately hard. (Most of these women were heroines!) A husband engaged in stock raising necessarily was away from home for considerable periods of time. There were no near neighbors, unless one would call someone living within a mile or two a near neighbor. Of "conveniences" as we understand the term colloquially, there were none.

As did all the women in the valley, Mrs. Williams bathed her children in the washtub with water heated by the wood-burning kitchen stove (often by candlelight), made most of their clothes herself, and gave them "home" remedies when they were sick. It was only when she deemed them in extreme danger that the doctor was called. On one occasion, when Jimmy was seven and Johnny four years old, there being no man on the ranch, she placed the two little boys on a none too gentle horse, Jimmy in the saddle and Johnny sitting behind the cantle holding to Jimmy, and told them to ride as fast as they could for a doctor. He was at Virginia City 12 miles away; the boys reached the doctor in an hour and a half, and he reached the ranch in about the same time; it took three hours to get the doctor, to say nothing of the peril to the little boys.

The Captain offered himself as a candidate for county commissioner in 1871 and was elected at the general election held in August of that year. This taste of public life whetted his appetite for more, and, perceiving the lucrative compensation of a sheriff, he sought that office and won the nomination without difficulty.

He resigned his office of county commissioner in June, 1873, and entered upon the campaign with confidence as a Republican; but the election of a Republican in territorial days was exceptional.

It was his misfortune to oppose at this election probably the best politician in the Democratic party of Madison County, Thomas J. Farrell, who had arrived in Alder Gulch in July, 1964. Mr. Farrell was an auctioneer, possessing unusual qualifications in that vocation. For a number of years he had been a familiar figure upon the streets of Virginia City on horseback calling auctions; in those days it seems they sold at auction about everything that was bought and sold in the community, even stocks of merchandise in the streets. By reason of this publicity, Mr. Farrell probably was better known to the people of Virginia City and vicinity than any other man. He was of a genial temperament, cordial in attitude, and a natural leader. After a hot campaign Farrell was elected. He said to me some years ago, "When I defeated Captain Williams, the big chief of the Vigilantes by four votes, I thought I was a sure enough politician."

In a narrative prepared by Mrs. Williams for delivery before the Pioneer Society, she also said Captain Williams was defeated by four votes; but an inspection of the records of Madison County shows that Mr. Farrell received 590 votes to Captain Williams's 570. This was the last adventure into politics that Captain Williams essayed. He continued to reside in his "house by the side of the road."

While Williams was a member of the board of county commissioners, the people of Virginia City and Madison County, anticipating that the city of Helena would continue its endeavors to secure the capital of the territory, an anticipation which was well founded, conceived the idea of building a courthouse in Virginia City sufficient to care for the territorial officers, believing that the possession of an adequate courthouse, which might be used as a capitol building, would be a strong factor in retaining the capital.

The project was carried out, ground was broken for the courthouse in the fall of 1873, and the erection of the structure went forward with commendable rapidity. The county jail was placed in the basement, and within the jail enclosure there was a steel cage, which at that time was supposed to be sufficient to hold the most desperate prisoner. After the cage was in place and in working order, Captain Williams hap-

"Virginia City, Montana Territory, 1877," by J. Ross Pollock. *Courtesy Lew. L. Callaway, Jr.*

pened to meet his old friend and boon companion, X. Beidler, deputy U.S. marshal in Virginia City. X. was addicted to playing practical jokes, such pranking being endemic in the early days of the territory. X. said, "Cap, I want to show you the new jail. It's a daisy."

The two proceeded to the jail, and X. induced the Captain to go into the cage with him to demonstrate some points of excellence in the steel work. As soon as the slow moving Williams was inside, X. slipped out and locked the door.

"Now," he said, "you old sinner, you can see how pleasant it is to be shut up. Stay there a while and see how those poor devils must have felt when you were bossing the Vigilantes."

Putting the key in his pocket, X. went downtown, saying to the boys that he had a new prisoner in the jail.

"By and by," he said, "I want you to go up and look at him."

The cage had not been furnished, and there was no place in the Captain's cell to sit except upon the floor; after he tired of standing up, he sat—in bad humor. In a half hour or so, X. collected some friends common to himself and Williams, about a dozen in number, and exhibited his captive with glee. After considerable "joshing" it was proposed that if the prisoner would "set 'em up" at the Pony saloon, he should be released. Williams agreed, but had to pay the fine two or three times before all were satisfied. Upon his return to the ranch he told Mrs. Williams of the occurrence and said, "The next time X. comes along here, I'm going to get even with him."

He did not have long to wait. X. had been on an expedition in Idaho, had made a long ride, and arrived at the Williams home about 5:30 in the evening. Mr. and Mrs. Williams were delighted to see him and asked him how far he had ridden. Was he tired? Was he hungry? He said he had ridden from the Blacktail, he and his mule were tired, he was cold, and he was hungry.

Williams said, "Well, you just go in the house and sit down and I'll put the mule away."

Mrs. Williams said, "I'll cook a good dinner."

She was a good cook, but slow, as X. knew. The boys were sent to the henyard to catch some young chickens.

"I'm about famished," X. said. "For goodness sake don't catch any chickens. Just put anything on the table you have."

"Oh, no, X.," replied Mrs. Williams. "When you come I always cook a good meal."

It took a long time to catch, dress, and cook the chickens; and supper was not ready until nearly eight o'clock. In telling about it afterwards, X. said, "By that time I could have eaten a pickled Chinaman."

Mrs. Williams knew the things X. liked and placed them on the table. He was a good eater and on this evening surpassed himself. In the meantime "Cap" had built a fire in the front room, and when X. left the table the heat, added to his over-stuffed condition, made it almost impossible for him to keep awake. Desiring to be polite, he endeavored to keep up the conversation for a time but found it impossible to do so.

"Cap," he finally said, "I've ridden a long way. I'm very tired. And I'm awfully sleepy. I hate to say so, but I wish you'd show me to my room."

"Oh," Cap said, "don't be in a hurry. Let's sit up and talk over old times."

"Yes," Mrs. Williams added, "You haven't been here for quite a while. We have lots to talk over."

X. struggled to keep awake, but occasionally nodded in spite of himself. Cap remembered the long moments he had spent in the cell, and with his wife's help kept poor X. in torture. Finally the Captain said, "Well, X., I guess it's time for you to go to bed. Wait until I get a lantern."

Having lighted a candle-lantern, he led X. across the road

to the corral, let down the bars, and the two stepped inside; then the Captain stepped outside and began to put up the bars.

"Well," X. said, "this is something new, ain't it, Cap? Where am I going to sleep?"

"Sleep with the other animals, you damned jackass," drawled the Captain, handing him the lantern.

X. went into the stable and collected some saddle blankets, made down his bed in a manger, and slept until morning. He arose early, but breakfast was awaiting him.

"How'd you sleep?" Williams asked. "I hope you were more comfortable than I was in that cell."

Life must have been hard for the Williams family in the latter 1870's. The only income was from the small herd of cattle and the sale of a horse now and then. As to crops, except for a good-sized garden, the ranch yielded only hay, but not more than was needed for the Captain's livestock. The family increased, but the family income did not. Prices for cattle and horses were low in '79, '80, and '81. All the ranchmen in the valley, except Alex Metzel, had to "figure close," to make ends meet. Mr. Metzel was a first-class cattleman and a natural money maker. While others were simply marking time, which most of them were compelled to do for want of resources, Metzel, taking advantage of the low market, purchased several hundred head of cattle, which he drove to Cheyenne, either to sell them there or ship them from that point. I do not remember which, but he netted a handsome profit. Incidentally, by this course he relieved an over-stocked home range.

CHAPTER EIGHT

Life on the Ranch with Williams and Callaway

Captain James Williams and Colonel James E. Callaway become ranch partners. The Montana cowboy and his gear. Captain Benteen's story of the Custer Massacre. Trouble with Indians. Bank robbery in Virginia City. The Chinese War in Alder Gulch.

IN 1881 my father, Colonel James E. Callaway, and Captain Williams decided to become ranch partners. Williams was to move to the Callaway ranch and the two were to run their herds as one. My father turned in 400 head of cattle and Williams, 105. They chose the circle on the left ribs for the company brand. All were pleased with the arrangement. I looked forward to happy associations with the Williams boys, and that anticipation was realized. But a temporary disappointment awaited me. I was told that I could not go to the ranch, which I loved, anymore, as I would be in the way there, that Captain and Mrs. Williams had boys enough as it was. My father said, as he had said before, "One boy's a boy, two boys half a boy, three boys no boy at all."

Here seems as good a place as any to speak of intimate affairs in the Williams family. In the everyday affairs of life Captain Williams was an easygoing man, good natured, a pleasant

Colonel James Edmund Callaway, secretary of the Territory of
Montana from 1871 to 1877 and ranch partner of Captain
James Williams. Courtesy of Lew. L. Callaway, Jr.

person to live with, indulgent with his family, and with those whom he employed. I recall one good example of his ease with growing boys. At the Callaway ranch Mr. and Mrs. Williams, the girls, and small children slept in the log buildings, while the large boys slept in the frame house. When the Captain arose, which was early in the morning, he would open the door of the frame house and say, "Get up, there, boys, and hear the birds sing," or, "Get up, you lazy devils, and help me pail the cows."

On the first occasion sometimes he would not receive any response at all, and upon the second a sleepy or lazy one. But when he came the third time, it was time to get up, no foolishness about it—we got up and hustled. This was the regular course, but, if he really meant business the first time, he came inside and told us to get up and stayed until we did. He was possessed of a whimsical sense of humor and at meal times frequently kept us laughing by telling stories but seldom talked of himself.

His wife was an excellent woman with a shrewish turn of mind. She was proud of her husband and children but was inclined to criticize them for their failure to do this or that. She laid stress upon culture, frequently criticizing her husband for his failure to provide educational advantages for the children, and at the same time scolding them for neglecting the opportunities which were provided. If the Captain took notice of this flow of language at all, his comment was mild, generally humorous; but the persistency of it worried him.

Whenever he had anything important to do, he avoided strong liquor; but at other times he was fond of it and imbibed freely. As he grew older this tendency grew upon him, and it was difficult for him to maintain sobriety upon his visits to Virginia City; he could not resist the temptation to drink with his old friends. On these occasions he would furnish his share of the entertainment by telling stories and occasionally singing.

It was intimated that if my conduct about home were satisfactory, I might be permitted to visit the ranch sometime during the summer. My dissatisfaction over the futility of life in town and persistent importunities concerning the promised visit must have worried my doting parents because they arranged for the "visit" immediately upon the close of school, the latter part of May. To my delight, Captain Williams told me he planned to take his boys, Jimmy and Johnny, and me with him "on the Blacktail round-up." The cattlemen in the Ruby had been advised by Poindexter & Orr, the famous pioneer cattlemen in the Blacktail Valley, that they had sold several thousand cattle to an English firm, which intended to drive the herd to Canada; and it was suggested that the Ruby people attend the roundup to look after their own.

The price of cattle had gone up; Poindexter & Orr sold to Major Walker, superintendent of the Cochrane Cattle Company, 6,000 head at $25, amounting to $150,000. The *Dillon Tribune* of May 27, 1882, reported "it is the largest sale ever made in this section of the Territory, and we believe, the largest cattle sale ever made in Montana. The cattle are to be driven to the Cochrane company's range on Bow River, 100 miles north of Fort McLeod, in the British possessions."

Adopting the kindly suggestion, a large number or Ruby Valley riders went to the Poindexter & Orr ranch by way of the old Salt Lake Road, which led up the Sweetwater and over the Big Hill. We found at the "P. & O." the largest aggregation of cowboys we had ever seen and were astonished over the outfits possessed by some of them, who evidently had spent large sums of money in purchasing the finest equipment to be had in the way of saddles, bridles, chaps, spurs, reatas, and the like. On the evening of our arrival we were told to turn our horses loose in the calf pasture, and when we inquired where that was they said, "Right here."

After stripping our horses and seeing them roll, we observed them disappearing over the nearby hills; we asked how large the calf pasture was, and somebody said, "It's about 10 miles square."

It may not have been quite that large, but it certainly did embrace a good many square miles. We camped for several days on that spot while the round-up was in progress, during which there was always a great deal of interest going on. We had our breakfast and horses saddled before sunrise. The mornings were chilly, and the horses unruly. Some of the performances at that early hour were very like a modern rodeo, but there were none of the casualties which accompany these modern exhibitions. Occasionally a rider was thrown, but not frequently. The spirit of mischief is always abroad in a cow camp, and practical joking was indulged in; but everybody was good-natured; to my knowledge there was not a quarrel.

Among the Canadians there were three stalwart young Englishmen, just over from the "old country," evidently the sons of those interested in the Cochrane Cattle Company. These young men were free spenders and they had bought everything the cowboys had recommended. Such "outfits" as the cowboys had persuaded them to buy, I fancy were never seen before or since. The good-natured English boys were the butt of all sorts of jokes perpetrated by the fun-loving cowboys. The jokes were fun for all but the Englishmen. Finally one of them, after being bucked off—the result of a "job"—into the Blacktail, which was running full, said it was a bit too thick and quit the round-up.

After sundown the group would gather around the campfires or in a large log bunkhouse and entertain one another by telling stories, singing, and the like.

Some of the boys sang the usual cowboy songs. Of course, somebody had to wail the lugubrious "Cowboy's Lament." Captain Williams had a good voice and liked to sing when the surroundings were to his liking. Upon this occasion he sang, "by request," "Tim Finnigan's Wake." It ran like this:

> Tim Finnigan lived in Walker Street
> A gintleman Irishman, mighty odd;
> He had a beautiful brogue that was rich and sweet
> And to rise in the wurruld he carried the hod.

There were a number of verses to this ditty, each followed by a chorus beginning:

> Hip hur rah ra! your souls to blazes!
> Welt the floor, your trotters shake!

But the next inspiring lines I am unable to remember.

He also sang a doleful ditty, reminiscent of the early days of Pennsylvania, concerning Amanda, who "was the pride of her village and home."

After the local cattle were cut out, the great drive began. It was difficult to start the huge herd, but after it was strung out the cattle pursued the usual course; the beef steers and other strong stock took the lead, while far back the older cattle and the cows with calves constituted the drag. It was necessary to restrain the lead and to keep it from spreading; so several experienced cowboys were assigned to that pleasant service. Two or three men rode ahead to restrain the leaders, and others rode along on either side to keep the cattle from straying. Between the lead and the drag two or three thousand moved along at an ordinary gait, with cowboys alongside. The dust increased as the herd proceeded. One who has not experienced it will never appreciate the hardship of "punching the drag."

The pace is very slow, and the dust insufferable. As the cattle tire, they attempt to break away. Cows turn around looking after their calves, the calves run every which way, and some recent arrivals "play out" and have to be carried in the wagon.

Of course, the boys were ordered to work on the drag. Those with the lead rode along easily, telling stories and singing songs. After riding with the drag for several hours, I tired of it; it did not seem good sense to me to stay with the drag if I could ride with the lead. Perceiving a yearling that seemed lively and about to break out of the herd, I kept close to her until she broke, and then, instead of driving her back into the drag, I pursued her up to the lead bunch where I stayed.

The Ruby riders went with the great herd until it crossed the ridge between the Blacktail and the Centennial. Returning to the Poindexter & Orr ranch, on the next day we took our cattle and drove home.

We were not bothered much with cattle thieves, but it was deemed prudent to brand your calves at first opportunity. We had a big branding day in June and branded from then on as the calves came. The fall roundup was principally for beef cattle. What great, broad-backed, rolling-with-fat steers they were—four, five, and even six years old. It was the policy of the cattlemen to hold their steers until they were four. This policy was too expensive as the years went on. As the expense of raising cattle increased, it became necessary to get quicker returns on the investment. Note the "baby beef" of the present time. The cattlemen had riders on the range continually, except in haying and in winter months, and rode frequently in the winter.

In the spring and in the fall the Metzel boys, Frank, (later sheriff of Madison County), Charley, Tom, Will, the Peterson boys (Sam and Ralph), Johnny Donegan, Bob Maloney, Jim and Johnny Williams, and myself were on the range pretty continuously. We knew each other every well and worked in cooperation. This was in the 80's. In those years there drifted in occasionally the cowboy from Texas and the southwestern plains. They came with the great herds that were driven along the Salt Lake Road and thence to different parts of Montana. As I said, these herds came down our valley. We called them "through herds." When we saw a great continuous dust coming down the Sweetwater, we took to horse. It behooved us to be present as the herd passed by. Those drivers were not careful to cut out local cattle. Many a one has been driven away with a through herd. We rode through the transient herds and cut out the local cattle, no matter whose. The drivers did not object. It would not have made any difference if they had. The local cattlemen would not suffer any interference with their rights.

A cowboy, fed up with the long trail, would drop out occasionally. If he were a good fellow, for a time he found himself lionized. His tales of the regions through which he had come, of the "cow-trails," his new songs, and up-to-date equipment were interesting. Occasionally an exceptional rider or expert pistol shot would show up. One, Tucker by name, was both. The hombre, as he sometimes referred to himself, frequently could put six bullets in a telegraph pole as he rode by on the lope. But, except for shooting, none came who was superior to the local boys in any respect. They threw the rope no better than we did, did not understand working with stock cattle as well as the local boys. As an "all-around cowhand" no one of them equalled Anson Caswell, or a dozen others I might men-

144

tion. None came who rode better than Charley Pendarvis or Bob Boatman or Frank Powers. In fact, nearly all local boys were good riders.

Everyone had a saddle, bridle, spurs, and quirt. Some had fancy bits, inlaid with silver, spurs the same. Some had tapaderos over their stirrups, in imitation of the southwestern riders. In the early 80's, chaps came in use. Tapaderos and chaps are essential in the southwest where the high cactus and the thorny shrubs are a constant menace. Our men found the tapaderos of little use, preferring the slender, open stirrup. But chaps were a veritable Godsend to the range rider. The leader sheds the rain and snow and protects from the wind. Some sported the chaps with angora goat fur, but most of the boys contented themselves with leather, generally with fringe. The usual clothing was of "overall" material, brown coats with wool lining, blue or brown trousers. While on the range, the cowboys wore a red silk handkerchief loosely about his neck, tied cravat style or in an ordinary knot. An odd practice was to wear ordinary cloth trousers and overall, the latter from two to four inches shorter than the trousers. If the overalls were not short enough, he folded them so that the trousers near his boots were unprotected below the overall.

The hat was felt, crown of average height with brim about four inches wide. Ten gallon hats and "bulldogging" are vaudeville stunts. A cowboy would have a fine time trying to bulldog one of our range steers three, four, or five years old. The saddle at first had a single cinch which was placed but a little back of the front legs, causing the saddle to ride well up on the horse's withers. The cinch frequently cut into the body near the legs. Next came the well known "double cinch," and then the "center-fire," which places the cinch well toward the middle of the horse's belly; still later came the "three quarter rig" in which the cinch is well back from the front legs but farther forward than the "center-fire." The "double cinch" and the "three quarter" justly became the favorites.

Books have been written about the cowboy. The fact is, fundamentally he was no different from the vigorous young American in any walk of life. His training made him superior in his particular calling. The average cowboy gloried in "playing it on the square" and did so. He swore, was rough in habit and demeanor, "lickered up" when he had the opportunity, was good at heart, and would go the limit for his friend. In all the years of my life in the Upper Ruby, I never witnessed a personal encounter between the cowboys. They would "cuss each other out" on occasion and the spectator would anticipate a fight sure, but there never was. It certainly wasn't for lack of courage. They must have had level heads.

I recall, however, one incident which occurred between my father and a man named "Rattlesnake Jack." We had gone on a roundup into the Sweetwater Basin. With us, of course, went the men from Blacktail who had been riding with us. There had been, and was, no disagreement. In the Basin other riders from the Blacktail joined us, among them a newcomer who was called "Rattlesnake Jack." He was a tall man, muscular, wearing a hat with a rattlesnake skin for a band.

About noon I began to hear discussion over an unbranded yearling, a heifer. The Ruby riders said she came from our side of the divide and belonged to our association, which would sell her at auction at the regular time. The Blacktail riders seemed to be agreeing with Rattlesnake Jack that they would take the heifer with their cattle to the Blacktail. My father, who was captain of the roundup that day, was appealed to and he said that according to the rules and agreement between the Ruby and Blacktail stockholders, the heifer belonged to us.

146

Then Rattlesnake became belligerent and abusive. My father got off his horse to tighten the cinch. As he did that, Rattlesnake Jack said something abusive. My father bore the reputation of being unafraid of anybody or anything, and it was known he was a fighter. He said, "I don't know you nor care who you are. If you are hunting trouble you can have it. Get down off your horse and I will fight you in anyway you choose and with any weapon. Now fight or shut up." He seemed to grow into the stature of a large man. Rattlesnake Jack said he wasn't hunting for a fight and that settled the affair. I never saw him again. Some time later a man bearing his name, "Rattlesnake Jack," was hanged at or near Lewistown. Whether he was the same man I don't know.

Another thing about cowboys is that every last one always respected a good woman. Indeed he possessed innately the chivalry of the knights of old. I remember, for instance, one time when there had been a dance at Puller Springs. An employee of our ranch went with his girl. The next day, about noon, four cowboys rode up to our stables. Seeing me one said, "Where's Red?" (That wasn't his name.)

"He's up Sweetwater."

"Well," said the spokesman, "we heard and we believe it's so that he gave Loretta (not her name) a drink of whiskey last night. If he does it again, we'll either tell her folks or we'll put a rope around his neck and throw him in the creek."

This was told to me for transmission. I passed the word.

The boys who grew up in the valley were not alone good cowboys. The necessities of their time and place compelled them to turn their hands to the everyday tasks of the ranchmen. They preferred to ride, of course, but they repaired ditches, irrigated the hay lands, built fences, put up hay, and got timber from the mountains, as the exigencies required.

"*Custer, Reno and Benteen with Gray Horse Troupe on Eve of Custer's Massacre,*" *by O. C. Seltzer. Courtesy of Gilcrease Instute.*

Captain Benteen's Story of the Custer Massacre

Although, as I said, we didn't have much trouble with cattle thieves, Indians were another story. In 1876 came Lieutenant General George A. Custer's defeat at the Little Big Horn. Many years later I chanced to hear a first-hand account of this incident.

After taking my entrance exams at the University of Michigan, Ann Arbor, Michigan, I went home to Virginia City and Jessamine Ranch to spend a glorious summer. En route I met Colonel Sanders at the depot in St. Paul. We took the same Pullman, and I enjoyed the ride. At Miles City we went out on the car platform to see who was there. There was, of course, a crowd to see the train come in.

Colonel Sanders saw a medium sized man in a grey suit and called, "Hello, Benteen!"

He replied, "How do you do, Colonel Sanders, I am going with you."

It was the celebrated Captain Frederick Benteen who had saved Reno's command at the Custer fight. He told Colonel Sanders he was going to the tenth anniversary of the fight at Fort Custer and then was going on to Fort McKenzie, I think it was, in Wyoming. Benteen had been a young colonel in the Civil War, with a fine record. He was the senior captain in the Seventh Cavalry at the battle of the Little Big Horn.

He had testified at the Reno court martial and was loath to say anything more about the battle. But Colonel Sanders was a mischievous man; he wanted to hear Benteen's story. Finding he could not get Benteen to talk of the battle, he began to criticize the conduct of the battle and to make outrageous statements.

Exasperated, Benteen said, "Colonel Sanders, you are too

Captain Frederick Benteen, senior captain of the Seventh Cavalry when General George Custer was in command. Courtesy of Montana Historical Society.

influential a man to make such mistaken statements; they are not true."

"Well," Sanders said, "that's the way I understand it; what are the facts? I don't care to misstate."

Then Benteen told us how the regiment came over the ridge from the Rosebud and into the valley of the Little Big Horn; how Custer sent him with three troops to scout to the left for the purpose of preventing the Indians from getting away to the east or southeast, Reno to go down the creek they were following and cross the river, striking the Indians at the upper end of the camp. Reno had three troops. Custer would take five troops and strike the Indians at the lower end. These were practically the same tactics Custer employed at the battle of the Washita. But Custer wasn't fighting five tribes[1] of the Sioux at the Washita, plus other hostiles.

Benteen marched with his three troops in a southerly direction. At one point they neared a clump of trees or brush, an ideal place for Indians to be in ambush. Benteen said he never was more scared in his life, and his soldiers felt the same way. But no one was there. Benteen's horses were tired after their night's march but they scouted the country pretty thoroughly. Satisfied there were no Indians in that part of the country, he turned to join Reno.

Before he reached Reno, he heard heavy firing and went forward on a trot. When they reached a stream, the horses were thirsty and drank despite efforts to get them across quickly. Crossing the stream they rode rapidly toward Reno. The firing was heavy and they soon came in sight of multitudes of warriors. They climbed the ridge where Reno was partially entrenched. Reno was lying on his back looking at the clouds.

---

[1] Estimated fighting Indians: eight to nine thousand. Edgar I. Stewart, *Custer's Luck* (Norman: University of Oklahoma Press, 1955).

He did not think Reno had been drinking, but he seemed unnerved. The troops were well deployed. All were fighting. Benteen took command.

Some officers thought the command ought to go to the relief of Custer; others thought such a move would be foolish. There were hundreds, if not thousands, of Indians in the valley. Reno had already lost heavily. Finally a charge was made, but the Indians were in too great force. The troop charging fell back to the entrenchments, such as they were. They dug with whatever they had to make rifle pits. Many were wounded and the need of water was acute. The next day, I think he said, they organized a party to go for water, supporting them by sharp fire. In this way they got some water.

They fought all the afternoon of the 25th, until dark, and from day break on the 26th until the middle of the afternoon, when they saw the Indians leaving the valley. The next morning Lieutenant Bradley, followed by General Terry, came up. This was the first word they had of Custer's fate.

Benteen left us at Custer Station.

In 1877 we heard the Nez Perce Indians were on the warpath. I remember my father telling my mother about the disastrous battle of the Big Hole.[2] In this battle a force of 155 officers and men of the 7th U. S. Infantry with 8 other soldiers and 36 citizen volunteers, under command of General John Gibbon, surprised and fought all day a superior force of 400 Nez Perce warriors (who had with them 150 squaws and children). More than one-third of the military command was either killed or wounded.

The Nez Perce were retreating through Montana on their way to Canada when this bloody engagement was fought. The

---

[2]G. O. Shields, *The Battle of the Big Hole* (New York: Rand McNally, 1889). The battle of the Big Hole, August 9 and 10, 1877, was 100 miles from Virginia City and 170 miles from Helena.

Nez Perce had long been a peaceful tribe living in eastern Idaho.[3] They left their reservation to seek sanctuary in Canada after some young "hot-heads" of their tribe murdered white men and women in Wallowa Valley, Oregon.

General O. O. Howard, commanding the Department of the Columbia, began a pursuit of the fleeing Indians; but from the beginning he was either bypassed or his forces defeated, as they were at the battle of the Big Hole.

Governor B. F. Potts of Montana ordered several civilian companies to be formed to assist General Howard in an effort to force the Indians to return to their reservation. My father, Colonel James E. Callaway, because of his fighting experience in the Civil War and the proximity of Virginia City to the line of march, was asked to raise a company to go to the assistance of General Howard. (Camas Creek, where Callaway's company caught up with General Howard was some fifteen miles southwest of Henry's Lake and about thirty miles west of Yellowstone Park.) The company was to be for the protection of the settlers. The settlers would have been safer without the army.

Callaway's company comprised some real Indian fighters and some good citizens who were willing to fight. Colonel Deimling, late colonel of the 10th Missouri; Sam Word, noted lawyer and orator; Sim Buford, leading merchant; Doctors Smith and Yager; Tom Baker, editor of the *Madisonian*; Tom Farrell, former Confederate soldier and sheriff; R. O. Hickman; William Morris, druggist and leading citizen; and Father Kellegher, Catholic priest, a good fellow and a fine marksman, went along. There were 40 men in the Company. Tom Farrell, part owner of a large horse ranch, furnished many horses. My father rode Chief, worth $150. He furnished another worth

[3] Other tribes of the Nez Perce lived in Oregon and Washington.

$175. Well I remember seeing the company going forth to war. Each man rode a horse. Everyone had a pistol and a gun. The mountain howitzer brought up the rear. They left town one fine August evening, the women in tears. They knew their husbands would be killed. My mother was sure my father would be. I felt injured because, being a small boy, I could not go; so I would not get a scalp. The company went out sixteen miles along the Salt Lake Road to the crossing of the Ruby, and then sent back for ammunition for the cannon; they had forgotten it. The invidious, who remained at home, said that wasn't the kind of ammunition they wanted. They must have run out of the necessary article pretty quick.

The company went on bravely, up Sweetwater and over the Big Hill, going down on the Blacktail side, their eyes alert for savage warriors; and they beheld them in large numbers. The Virginians halted, held an impromptu council of war. My father, the captain, decided to charge. When in danger, attack! All who had been in the army favored that course over intrenching. Spurs were put to the horses and the charge was on. But it was only a large band of horses going to water!

General Howard was reported marching to Camas Creek. My father sent a courier to the general, tendering the services of his company. I have the bacon-grease stained message. It was written from Camp Sladen, Headquarters Department of the Columbia. The general addressed my father by his army title, colonel, and said he would be glad to have the assistance of his command. He said he would not promise a battle tomorrow, but would do all in his power "to bring about that highly desirable result." The general's army lay along Camas Creek in Idaho. My father was directed to camp just across the creek, to turn his horses in with the army horses, and was advised that the army sentries would surround the entire camp. My father objected. He said his horses were acquainted and would stay together; also, that some of his men knew Indians and would be excellent on sentry duty. Now, horses are gregarious and they do not make up with strange horses at once. But "orders is orders," and the general had his way.

The volunteers from Virginia City made up their beds and went to sleep. Now comes an odd occurrence. It had been reported to General Howard that there was a canyon through which the Indians must pass, beyond Henry's Lake, in which a troop of cavalry could intrench, blocking the way. The main army coming up would entrap the Indians; it would be repetition of Thermopylae if they didn't surrender. So Lieutenant Bacon was sent ahead with his troops to block the canyon. When Bacon got to Henry's Lake he found the country full of passes, none of which he could block. He sent word by his Indian scouts to Howard, telling of the conditions he found and saying he was returning to join the main command. At least, that was the story as everyone understood it. The Indian scouts, Bannacks, must have leaked the information. The Bannacks and Nez Perces were pretty friendly. The soldiers knew Bacon was returning.

In the morning about daybreak, the sleepy sentinels saw Bacon and his troops returning, or thought they did. They came in columns of fours. As the column came close, the sentries challenged, and bedlam seemed to break loose. There were war whoops, guns firing, blankets waving, as the Indians rode through the volunteers' camp and across the creek, cutting off Howard's horses and the volunteers.

The volunteers got out of their blankets in a hurry and began to fire their guns. They ran toward the main command; some found shallow fords, others deep holes—notably Sam Word who was six feet tall. Only his whiskers appeared above the water. Doctor Yager, running, stepped on the end of a stick which struck his other leg, throwing him to the ground.

He yelled, "My God, I'm shot!" Doctor Smith, the other surgeon, ran to him but didn't find any bullet wound. No one was hurt. It was called the Camas Creek Massacre. Daylight came. The army was afoot—all but Captain Norwood's troop. He had but recently arrived, and his horses wouldn't associate with the army horses. Upon the attack the bugler blew "Boots and Saddles," upon which Norwood's troopers mounted and rode to "Frying Pan" Basin, where there was a real fight. The volunteers from Virginia City claimed that some of them went to the basin, offering substantial aid to Norwood's command.

Doctor Smith, a highly intelligent man, understood the Nez Perce tongue. He told the army officers he heard the great voice of Looking Glass above the din, giving commands. Hearing what the great chief said, the officers said his commands would not have been any more perfect if he had been graduated from West Point.

The volunteers eventually arrived home afoot, all but Tom Baker who had tied up his horse, the Morris boys' pet, "Old Baldy." Anybody could stir up a fight by mentioning the massacre at Camas Creek. During the winter the wags forgot it and peace reigned.

It was reported in Virginia City just after the "battle" that a man had been killed. The bugler was killed, and, I think, there were some killed in Frying Pan Basin. All the women in Virginia claimed "the man." My mother was sure it was my father. "He was so brave," she said.

He looked like a mountain man when he did return. His clothes were rough and travel-stained. He didn't have much to say about the Camas Creek affair.

Before it is too late, I must tell of something very few white people now living ever saw: a scalp dance by Indians on the warpath. The Indians were constantly about Virginia City, some secretly hostile, but most peaceable. It was usual for them to camp east of town but in the city limits, which were undefined by marks. To be more specific, they camped east of the slaughter house. That was convenient because there was wood, water, and grass, and they were able to procure heads of beef and entrails which they ate. At least they ate parts of them.

Will Thompson (a famous multi-millionaire to be), Will Demling, another boy whose name I don't recall, and I were up Gumpatch Hollow (Holler). Seeing a new Indian camp on the little stream, which I suppose you would call the lefthand fork of Daylight Creek above the slaughter house, we went to it but not too close to the camp. The way the Indians acted we thought they were not too friendly. We sat upon the hill above the camp. It was near sundown and we should have been at home. I don't know what month is was but it must have been summer. This makes me believe it was 1877, for we were on the Ruby most of the summer in 1878.

The occurrence is clear in my memory. The Indians were having some sort of ceremony. Some of the squaws were sitting around making a circle. They had drums, made, it seemed to me, of skins stretched on narrow tubs. They pounded on these with instruments that looked like coup sticks. The bucks marched into the circle nearly naked, no blankets—we were used to seeing them in blankets. They were painted in various colors, mostly black. There were white and yellow stripes. The squaws were painted, too, red predominating. The bucks had long poles with scalps dangling from the tops. The scalp must have covered an entire head. The bucks began to go around in a sort of mincing step which accelerated, the knees going up as high as the waist. They yelled "high yah hah, high ya hah," and other exclamations interspersed with the war whoop. This was made by loud yells, while clapping their hands to their mouths. This went on for a long time, faster and faster.

It was an interesting but not a terrifying exhibition to us. As it grew into twilight, we boys went home. We were astonished that our parents seemed terrified when we told them what we had seen. Of course, we were scolded, and I believe Will Thompson was "licked" for being so late. We were told to keep a long way from Indian camps. I do not believe we were in danger. We were little boys near a town full of fighting men. The scalp dance was undoubtedly a demonstration preparatory to going to war with an unfriendly tribe; maybe they were only going to steal horses.

Conditions were none too good on the Bannack Indian Reservation in the winter of 1877–78. The government had not kept its promises, and there was much dissatisfaction among the Indians. There was some violence. Notwithstanding this, peace was maintained by the Bannacks under their chief Tendoy as tribal policy.

In 1878 the Ruby Valley fell victim to a Bannack-Nez Perce raid. Undoubtedly it was because of the number and quality of its horses that the Indians selected it for their depredations.

It was the most exciting time the valley had ever known. During Chief Joseph's passage through Idaho and southwestern Montana, a number of his warriors, too badly wounded to travel, laid up for repairs with the Bannacks. The tribe had been friendly to the whites for a number of years. The main body under Tendoy remained so. But is is fair to say that after the battle of the Big Hole, where Indian women and children were killed in their beds, the Indians in our part of the country were fearful and resentful. Should we blame them?

When the so-called renegade Nez Perces and Bannacks determined to go horse stealing, no one knows. At one time they must have contemplated something more serious than mere horse stealing. Some time before the raid there were more than the usual number of Indians in our valley. That some of them planned considerable deviltry is shown by the following, and here the narrative becomes somewhat personal to me.

I was a good rider for my age, nine years. I frequently went to Puller Springs, two miles distant, for the mail and was often dispatched into the nearby hills for cattle. One morning about ten o'clock I was sent up to Jessamine or "Dry Creek" to look for some cows which had failed to come home the night before. My trip consumed about two hours, as I went well beyond the head of the creek.

About eleven o'clock, fifteen or twenty Indians pitched camp at a point easterly from our ranch buildings, where they had a good view of the valley. This was strange, as before the Indians had always camped in the river bottom near water. My father and mother were alone at the house; the two hired men were away on some duty. My father made a remark concerning the unusual Indian camp. Soon two Indians, a buck and a squaw, approached the ranch on foot. The squaw went into the kitchen where my mother was and in an insolent manner demanded something to eat. My mother was not inclined to accede, but my father signalled her to comply with the request. The buck and my father stood and talked, then sat down on the edge of the porch and continued their conversation. The occasion seemed to call for watchfulness and my father used his eyes. It was well he did, for through a lucky parting of the Indian's blanket he saw the brave about to draw a huge knife from its scabbard. Colonel Callaway was noted for his coolness in the face of danger. Rising slowly, as if observing something across the nearby river, and as soon as he could use his legs for that purpose, he sprang away from the Indian and into the house. He "made it in two jumps." Grabbing his needle gun, he told the squaw to "get out and get out quick," and, cocking the gun, he ordered Mr. Buck Indian to take his squaw and go and said that if any Indian was seen coming from that camp he would shoot and shoot to kill.

Buck and squaw both made hasty tracks to their camp. Then my parents, particularly my mother, began to worry about me. I should have been back long before. But in a little while I came across the bench, on the lope, two hundred yards from the Indian camp. Told of the episode with the Indians, I expressed keen regret that I was not present to see my dad make them skedaddle. Colonel Callaway always believed that if he and my mother had fallen victims that day, a general massacre would have followed that would have embraced all of the scattered ranches there.

It was not long after this incident that riders warned the settlers of a war party coming swiftly. There was great commotion upon the ranches. The men took their wives and children to Puller Springs, then went back to guard their buildings, horses, and cattle. A goodly number of cowboys and horse-wranglers were at Puller Springs. The women and children were safe, absolutely safe. No Indian would take a chance against the aggregation at Puller Springs.

We went to the Springs in the middle of the afternoon. I rode my saddle horse, Charley; I wasn't going to risk him at the ranch. It was fun to see other people arriving. They came in a hurry. Everybody wanted to fight. The women wanted to stay with their husbands and fight. About four o'clock there was a great dust up the road; from this emerged a team, and it certainly was coming. When it dashed up to the hotel, you could scarcely tell the color of the horses for foam. It was Hillhouse Raymond's fastest team, driven by a trusty man, bringing Mrs. Lane and child from Belmont Park. She told a graphic story of how, when Mr. Raymond had news of the oncoming savages, he sent his riders to the range for the mare band and his most valuable geldings.

Among the riders were two colored boys recently from Kentucky, and they had heard of Indians and what Indians would do to a man. The riders got to the horses but little ahead of the Indians, and then there was a race for the corrals at Belmont Park. The colored boys rode like devils; they guided the lead and went into thes corrals with the lead, too. (They started back to Kentucky that same week.) The last of the horses beat the Indians into the corral by not over 50 feet. Then Raymond and his men with rifles and shotguns halted the Indians. The situation was ticklish. If a shot had been fired no one knows what would have happened. But all kept their heads. The Indians threatened but finally went away. But they got many of Raymond's valuable horses from the adjacent range.

That night there were huge signal fires on the mountains, telling the Indians which way to go. They came down the Sweetwater to near its junction with the Ruby, then followed the river toward its course, probably dropped into the Centennial (Red Rock) Valley, crossed that and then the main range of the Rockies into Idaho. On the way they got hundreds of horses in the Ruby. Everybody lost good horses. They took one of our saddle horses, "Old Charley," from our field within 100 feet of our ranch houses. But they did not molest a person or a house on their raid. Their scouts undoubtedly had seen the preparations for defense. These were not extensive, but effective. Take ours for example. There were three men at our ranch. My father guarded the houses; Broadhead, a trustworthy and courageous colored man, guarded the stables; and Bill O'Neill, who was a fighter, from the vantage point of the chicken coop kept vigilant eyes upon the sheds and corrals. Similar guards were at the other ranches.

The Indians whooped horribly, but they did not take any chances. Generally Indians will not attack white men in ambush. It was nevertheless an anxious night for everybody, especially for the women. Visions of scalped husbands obtruded, and the bedbugs at the hotel were numerous and busy. The bedbugs fought all night and so did we. Our illuminations were candles. The ceiling of the bedrooms was unbleached muslin upon which the trademark appeared at intervals in blue print. Occasionally a bedbug would ascend the walls, crawl along the ceiling, and drop down on the bed. You ask any old-timer whether bedbugs did that! My mother just loathed bedbugs. She couldn't sleep a wink. She said fervently, "I wish I was at home with your father fighting those Indians."

The hotel was of logs, as I have said, but the partitions were of one-inch plank, which fitted together none too closely. The walls, like the ceiling, were covered with muslin. The acoustic properties throughout the hotel were good! We heard others engaged in battle with the bedbugs.

Morning dawned. The Indians and horses were gone. Peace reigned in the quiet, beautiful valley.

But the day was a busy one. The ranchmen organized a party, armed with needle guns and Winchesters, to follow the Indians and to recover the horses. The party went above the canyon and followed the trail without difficulty. They rode hard but did not see an Indian, did not recover a horse.

BANK ROBBERY IN VIRGINIA CITY

On the sleepy noon of July 30, 1879, three men rode up to Henry Elling's bank in Virginia City. One held the horses and

The Henry Elling Bank, scene of the bank robbery in Virginia City, Montana, 1879 Courtesy of Montana Historical Society.

the other two went in. Shortly, the two men came out and walked down Van Buren Street to Cover Street, mounted, and loped up the road toward the slaughter house. I saw them, all three, as they went by the Hamp. Johnson stone house. About the same time down Wallace Street I heard cries of "Help!" It was A. J. Bennett in front of the bank. His hands were tied. He was yelling, "Help! Three men have robbed Elling's bank!" People began to run out of their business houses, guns in hand.

Mr. Bennett had been in the bank alone. When the two

164

came in, they commanded him to hold up his hands, which he did. Then one of the robbers tied Bennett's hands behind him with buckskin string and remained with Mr. Bennett while the other went in the vault. The robbers took all the money they could see and asked Bennett for more. He told them they had it all except the silver. There were two bags of silver containing $1,000 each, which they did not trifle with, but at the time there was about $75,000 in a drawer in the safe in the vault, which the robbers overlooked; also $200,000 in bonds and $20,000 in gold dust. The robbers took about $6,000 in all.

After warning Mr. Bennett to keep quiet and not give any alarm for fifteen minutes or they would kill him, they left. But he managed to get the door open almost immediately, though the buckskin cut into his flesh, and began yelling. The men of the town, after some futile shooting, took to horse, going into the hills to catch the robbers. They were well armed and had plenty of rope. But the robbers had already passed out of sight.

My father and his friend Jacob H. Baker a boot and shoe merchant, interested in horses and ranches also, went together. My father rode "Old Sam," a white or grey pacing horse, and Jake rode a big bay. Both had rifles. They thought it was likely that the robbers would go by the lakes. They made all speed to Butcher Gulch and there followed the stream to the lakes. They scouted the country thoroughly, as they thought, but seeing no one came back to Virginia City. The robbery was, of course, the subject of conversation in the entire Madison Valley. People in the valley suspected a young man named George Wells. He was gone from the valley that day and was evasive when asked as to his whereabouts. People went to the ranch where George had been staying. There some bright fellow dug in the chaff in the manger of a stable and found an oyster can in which there were bills aggregating

$500. George was arrested. He denied his guilt, but in default of bail had to lie in jail. X. Beidler happened in town and the rumor was that he arranged for a stool pigeon. Whether Beidler's doing or not, a man was put in jail with Wells on some trumped-up charge and pretended he would plead guilty when the court convened. Wells told him that he was the man who held the horses for the robbers who gave him the $500.

In the meantime, after his arrest, he had retained my father to defend him. All he had was a fine Sharps rifle, a double-action revolver of the latest make, and a saddle and bridle. These he gave my father. The Sharps is in our home in Helena.

After Wells told his story to the stool pigeon, the jig was up and he pleaded guilty, drawing a sentence of ten years. Now, that should end the story, but it does not. The next year my father was at Miles City as special United States attorney. His chief duty there was to prosecute horse thieves and men of that ilk. People were always stealing from the government. Fort Keogh was nearby. Miles City was a frontier town and a wild one. The town was full of saloons. A photograph at that time would have shown ox-teams, mule-teams, frontier wagons, horses tied to hitching posts in front of the business places, (especially the saloons), and men in frontier garb, Indians in blankets, and the general run of people one saw in that period along the streets.

After a hard day in court, my father and a friend strolled into a large saloon in which there were billiard tables, gambling paraphernalia, and the usual card and drinking tables. He and a friend seated themselves at a table and ordered a drink. In a little while his friend excused himself. Just as the gentlemen left, a lull occurred in the usual noise, and my father heard three rough-looking men talking at the adjoining table.

One said, "You got off pretty lucky at that; you didn't have to kill anybody." The other said, "It wasn't so good. We only got $6,000. We had to give a thousand of it to the feller who held the horses. We heard afterwards that the cashier had lied to us. There was $75,000 in another drawer. We didn't have to kill anybody, that was lucky, but we had a close call. Above the town a ways is some lakes. It was upgrade and the horses were blowed. We rode across a little creek in a quakin' asp grove and loosened the cinches. Then we laid down in the grass with our guns. Jest about that time we seen two men comin'. They had rifles and ropes. I guess they were lookin' for us. One was a big red-whiskered man on a bay horse and the other was a little man, ridin' a white pacer. The little man was tellin' the big man a story. They didn't see us. If they had, we'd had to shoot 'em. They rode past. They was the only two we seen."

My father said to himself that he needed some fresh air and he went outside.

That spring of 1881 we heard there was war between the Chinese down the gulch, four companies against two. The two were intrenched in cabins, the four attacking. Chinese bought nearly all the ammuniton in town, fired (people said) 10,000 shots, and no one was even powder burnt. The main road ran down Alder Gulch. The war was below Water Gulch. The bullets were flying so fast the traffic was diverted up Water Gulch and over the early day road through the hills to the Ruby Valley.

After all this it was found that one man had been killed by stabbing and another, breaking away from the beseiged, was run down past the mouth of the gulch and to the flat to the south, where a pursuer caught him and cut off his head. Finally, the sheriff's force put a stop to the war and arrested some Chinese. There was a trial before the probate judge, sitting as a committing magistrate. The Chinese lied like Ananias. Practically all of them could speak English but everyone had to have an interpreter. The interpreter undoubtedly did some of the lying. The lawyers, my father being one, were nearly distracted. It was charged by each side that the other was lying; that the respective interpreters were mis-representing. All of which charges were well founded. All witnesses had been sworn according to law. Much the Chinese cared about that. They were sworn on a Bible. Less, if anything, they cared about that. Then they went into the jailyard where they cut off a rooster's head and swore the witnesses according to the Chinese custom. That didn't seen to help much, if any.

Eventually, two of the defendants, Ah Wah and Ah Yen, were bound over to the district court. When the court convened, the great lawyer, E. W. (Warren) Toole appeared to assist the district attorney. My father and Judge Blake appeared for the defendants. My recollection is that Colonel Sanders also appeared for the defendants at some point in the proceedings. During the trial all the bizarre incidents of a trial in which Chinese are the principal witnesses occurred. One of the jurors fell sick. Mr. Toole and Judge Blake were willing to continue with eleven jurors. My father said he would accept the eleven jurors if he could, but his view was that it could not be done; the defendants had a constitutional right to a jury of twelve men in a capital case.

The judge decided that it was permissible, in the circumstances, to proceed with eleven men. The jury found the defendants guilty of murder in the first degree, which meant hanging. The defendants appealed to the supreme court of Montana which reversed the judgment and ordered a new trial. It had taken a long time to go from the district court to the supreme court. The defendants remained in jail. In the meantime an election was held and there was a change in sheriffs. The case came on for a new trial. A new judge appeared on the bench, and a new district attorney. The judge inquired if the People were ready. The district attorney said they were. Judge Blake said the defendants were ready. My father said, facetiously, that it was usual to have the defendants in court for their trial. The Court said, "Mr. Sheriff, bring in the defendants." The sheriff said he had brought in all the Chinamen held as prisoners. My father said, "These men are not Ah Wah and Ah Yen." Judge Blake said, "No, these are not the defendants."

The fact was that at some time, either in the term of the old sheriff or in the term of the new, two Chinese came in as visitors and stayed, and the two defendants walked out. So far as I know, the defendants were never seen in Virginia City again. Whether they were guilty no one knows.

Within a year or two after Williams & Callaway formed their partnership, they entered upon a plan to extend the scope of their ranching operations. Cattle were increasing upon the range, and it was clear that it would be necessary to feed more or less extensively to bring the herds through the winter; the preceding hard winter, 1880–81, had conclusively demonstrated that. Captain Williams took up two tracts of land through the exercise of privileges extended by the national government, and Colonel Callaway exercised his timber-culture right. Additional water was appropriated and ditches were dug to irrigate more land. Upon one ambitious project I acted as rodman for three weeks in the summer of 1883 under Surveyor C. W. Mead, who surveyed a ranch from the Jack Creek bench to near the mouth of the upper canyon. This was an irksome job for a boy who wanted to be with his companions on horseback in the constantly alluring pursuit of riding the range; but the experience was found beneficial in many ways in the succeeding years—it was useful to me after I became district judge and constantly had ditch problems before me in water-right litigation. Everything one learns is likely to be helpful at one time or another. The big ditch project fell through, but by means of the other ditches the partners put land under cultivation as fast as their means would permit.

After the hay was put up and the grain cut and shocked in the fall of 1883, the Captain said we boys had worked pretty hard all summer and he would reward us by taking us on a hunting trip above the canyon. This announcement, as may be supposed, was greeted with great enthusiasm. He arranged the details himself and went with us; he drove the team while we rode horseback; he did practically all the work except caring for the horses. We had to do that, to keep the horses on good grass and securely picketed, which was essential as they were always trying to get away.

Camp was pitched at Cottonwood, a clear, roaring stream. It was an almost ideal camping place, with plenty of good wood, and to the west ample bottom land covered with good grass. Grouse went right along the creek, and plenty were secured before dark.

The evening we made camp was warm, but it began to cloud up, and the wind raised; before morning it began to rain and then snow. Big game came close; Captain J. H. Davis and Charley Pendarvis killed two large elk within a mile of our camp. Despite the hardship of wet and cold, we boys enjoyed going to the scene of the kill and helping back the meat to the hunters' cabin which was just across the river. All the while the Captain stayed in camp. I am sure he would rather have been at home—he was enduring discomfort that others might have enjoyment. We returned to the ranch with elk, grouse, and ducks, feeling very much like successful hunters.

The opening of school called me to Virginia City, but I was back on the ranch next March. At that time the hillsides sloping from the benchlands to the valley floor were showing the effects of an overstocked range; carcasses of cows unable to withstand the winter were much in evidence, and from then on, until the new grass had attained a good stand, more cows died, some in spite of all efforts to save them. We saved some, but not many, by carrying hay, grain, and water to them. It was discouraging to the cattleman from a financial standpoint, and it wrung his heart to see the poor creatures die.

That year efforts to produce more fodder were redoubled; more grain was sown, more hayland irrigated. Everybody was busy. While we boys were not driving cattle from the poison patches on the Sweetwater, we were irrigating and repairing breaks in the irrigating ditches; the ditches were comparatively new and it seemed that any little thing would break them; gophers burrowed in the banks, livestock crossing in numbers would tramp down the lower sides, an old badger hole beneath the ditch bed would furnish an outlet for water, which is always trying to escape. Indeed, there's always plenty to do on a ranch. The year 1884 was good. The calf crop was excellent. After the spring round-up during which the calves were branded, the main herds were taken above the canyon.

As the summer came on, it was perceived that the crops were to be bountiful; we put up more hay than ever before and raised from 80 to 100 bushels to the acre on the 16-acre tract planted to oats.

CHAPTER NINE

Terrible and Disastrous Winter
of 1887

Cattle sold at $20 a head. Mild winters of 1885–86. Terrible winter of 1887. The herds wiped out. Captain Williams commits suicide.

LIFE, pleasant for us boys, received an added zest, for in 1884 a personage came to live with us. Someone told us a man was planting trees on Colonel Callaway's "timber culture," and at the first opportunity we stopped to talk with him. He was a medium-sized man, but strongly built, with greying hair and whiskers, a crooked nose, and blue-grey eyes; he said his name was Tom Robinson; when asked from whence he came, he changed the subject. He seemed disinclined to talk, and we were not much interested. A few days after this interview the Captain said he had arranged to have the fellow help in haying; when he came he insisted upon sleeping in the stable. At table he maintained an almost complete silence.

We feared he would be a poor companion, but this was soon dispelled; he was loquacious, had a marvelous memory, and was a good story teller. We soon found that while he was a native of Canada, born near New London, he had gone to Wisconsin as a youth, being employed in the lumber woods

172

when the war broke out. He enlisted, he said, "in the Sixth Wisconsin Volunteer Infantry, First Brigade—'the Iron Brigade,' First Division, First Army corps, Army of the Potomac—the Iron Brigade consisted of the Second, Sixth, and Seventh Wisconsin, and Ninteenth Indiana and the Twenty-fourth Michigan."

He talked of Bragg, Doubleday, Meredith, and in fact all of his brigade commanders, as if he knew them personally. He saw General Reynolds killed on the first day of Gettysburg. He was himself wounded at Antietam, Gettysburg, and in the Wilderness, and great scars upon his body and legs bore evidence of savage wounds. I knew a good deal of the history of the Army of the Potomac at that time (my father had a book bearing that title which I had devoured) and have read considerable on the subject since. It has always been a marvel to me how a private, an unlearned man, could have known as much about the grand strategy of the campaigns, as well as of the details of the great battles fought between the Army of the Potomac and the Army of Northern Virginia, as Tom Robinson knew; and he told us day after day of the intimate life of the soldier in the ranks, in the hospitals, and on furlough.

Then came a hiatus in his life history which he never told, ending with his arrival on the Yellowstone about 1875. He was employed for a considerable period by Hoskins & McGirl at or about Coulson on the Yellowstone (but McGirl could not remember any man during that period named Tom Robinson, nor one named Isaac Gillespie, which was the name of this man when he was a private in the Sixth Wisconsin). In 1876 he was a scout and courier for General Terry, and he was on the Custer battlefield on the morning of June 27, 1876, arriving almost simultaneously with Lieutenant Bradley, with his Indian scouts; Tom always claimed his mission was to deliver a message from Terry to Custer. He helped bury the dead, but as should be known by this time, the dead, except a very few, were not buried until much later.

During the years following, Tom was a buffalo hunter, employing skinners; he was a fine shot, but I think he drew the long bow when he told us of his kills; and for some years he was a trapper.

Why did he come to our country in such secrecy? Tom's knowledge of ranch work was comprehensive; he could do almost anything; and he was a tireless worker. His principles were good; none but good advice and admonitions came from Tom. Mrs. Williams wondered why he was a drifter; why he had come on foot and almost in rags. We found out after Tom had worked four or five months; he drew his wages, went to Virginia and drank steadily until every cent was gone, and then he returned sick and dispirited. It was a part of his life story; no dog returned to his vomit with greater persistency. But his companionship gilded the gold of a wonderful summer; each boy schemed for a place in the hayfield and about the ranch that would keep him with Tom. But Tom was no good on the range, and when the fall round-up started, we left him to grovel on the ranch while we reveled in the free life of a range rider.

In passing, I should say that after harvest the Captain again took us boys above the canyon, and we again camped at Cottonwood. This time the weather was glorious, game plentiful, life pleasant; the Captain again tended camp. He was no game hog; he insisted that we should not kill too many grouse. When he thought we were getting too many, he made us go fishing; and when he thought we had enough game and fish, said it was time to go home.

The country above the canyon is charming in middle September; frost visits the locality with the advent of that month, and nature paints the landscape with its lovely autumn colors;

mountain, hillside, and valley contribute to the beauty of the spectacle; at sunrise and sunset especially the views are glorious.

I shall always remember the fat cattle we brought to the corrals that fall. At that time it was not unusual to find six and five-year-old steers on the range. It was the policy to keep a steer until he was four years old; but people who needed money had to sell their "threes" and sometimes their "twos."

After the round-up was over, Williams & Callaway drove 60 head of fours, threes, and a few twos to Alex Metzel's where they were sold for $20 a head all around. Unknown to me, this was an indication that Williams & Callaway were in sore need of cash.

I bade good-bye to Captain Williams and his family during the forepart of December, and was not to see them again until June, 1886, spending the interval in attending school in Philadelphia in preparation for college. After passing the entrance examinations of the University of Michigan at Ann Arbor, I returned home. Nature had been kind to the stockmen in my absence. The winter of '85 and '86 was mild; and to those who believe the climate is changing, a letter written by Captain Williams to Colonel Callaway will be of interest. It also throws a light upon Captain Williams's character and illustrates a fight he was making against the wiles of John Barleycorn. Here it is:

Jessamine Ranch Jan 31 1886.

Col

Dear Sir

Sold the steers 3 yrs old over to Butte Bucher for $40.00 head, all that we can find in a limited time. Donegan Newbery and Smapp also sold Dont think will find them all as they are badly scattered.

No snow on range have nearly all the feed on hand yet. Joined the Good Templars last knight will never drink another drop of whiskey as long as I live unless I get snake bit I will not look for a snake either

Yours &ct

Cap

But a few days elapsed after my arrival before my father told me to go to the ranch, as additional help was needed.

A change had come upon the scene; the country above the canyon had been settled up. There had come into the valley a man named Bryant with a wife and many children, some of whom were grown. Some of the girls were married, and a grown son had a wife and family. All of these settled above the canyon. Bryant himself took up the ranch formerly occupied by Charles Leyendecker, which he began at once to improve. It is now the property of William Marshall. The young men took up all of the available land, and the people below the canyon were advised that the fence which had been thrown across the canyon to hold the cattle would not be respected.

The arrival of Bryant and his numerous family was not at all welcome, as may be supposed. He was a tall, broad, grey-haired and grey-whiskered man, with black eyes. Some wag called him Zip Coon, and the name stuck. But there were no unfriendly acts on the part of the older settlers, or the Bryants; on the contrary there was an honest attempt to "get along."

It was clear that additional range must be had. It was known that just over the divide which separates the headwaters of the Ruby River from the Red Rock there was a great valley, which bore the name of the Centennial, a portion of which had been used for ten years by the Poindexter & Orr people and Joseph Shineberger; but the great upper end of the valley was unoccupied.

So it was concluded to drive the Ruby Valley cattle to the Centennial in charge of an adequate number of cowboys. The Centennial derived its name from this circumstance: in 1876 Poindexter & Orr drove a considerable portion of their herds to the Red Rock Valley, about 20 miles easterly from Lima, being the first to occupy it, and gave it the name of Centennial. The valley is, roughly speaking, about 50 miles in length and from 10 to 15 in width. The Red Rock River runs through the Centennial from east to west. Its longest tributary, which comes out of Alaska basin, is the ultimate headwater of the great Missouri, and from its source to the Gulf of Mexico it is the longest stream in the world. At the upper end of the valley are the Red Rock lakes, two considerable bodies of water. The Ruby cattle were ranged about the Red Rock on either side and for some miles down the river, but well above those of Poindexter & Orr.

On the southerly side of the valley the main range of the Rockies rises somewhat perpendicularly; on the northerly side there are the rolling hills of the divide between the Red Rock and the Ruby, with the high Snow Crest and the Tobacco Root ranges toward the north. It was about 60 miles from our ranch to the cowboys' camp on the south side of the river, they being camped not far from where Lakeview is now. Naturally, I was anxious to see the great valley and to join the cowboys there. The opportunity came in the latter part of August when the Captain told Jim and me that it would be necessary to take a load of supplies to the boys in the Centennial; we were to go, assist in riding herd, and to remain until the fall branding was done.

The trip over was not an easy one with a loaded wagon and two saddle horses, neither of which led very well. The road from Lazy Man's Creek to the forks of the Ruby was difficult. For 30 miles or more it was a mere cow trail, and in places very sideling. In two places we stood on the upper side of the wagon to keep it from tipping over but made the trip without accident. When we topped the rise which gave me a first view of the Centennial Valley, I saw for the only time in my life a great valley of Montana as it was in its primitive state; there was not a habitation nor a fence to be seen.

Indeed, as I remember, there was not a fence from the head of the valley (unless it was that which enclosed a small garden on O'Dell Creek where a man of that name had recently located) for a distance of 40 miles down the valley. An Irishman, whose name I have forgotten, had begun the erection of a log cabin some miles below our camp.

Jim told me of the great number of ducks, brants, geese, and swans which would be found on the lower Red Rock Lake and the river, and he did not exaggerate it. We crossed the river at the Lousy Spring ford and drove up the sluggish river on its southerly side, talking of the odd color of its waters. As we came in sight of the water where it broadened and hardly appeared to move, I said to him, "That certainly is curious looking water."

"That isn't water," he answered, "that's ducks."

The truth is that for a space that covered a half acre or more the water could not be seen for the wild fowl. I believe the ducks and geese along that river and upon the lakes at that time would have run into hundreds of thousands. Red Rock Lake is still a favorite spot for duck hunters, but it differs vastly from what it once was.

At least 5,000 antelope were then ranging the Centennial Valley. One could see antelope at any time of day and, as one rode about the widely scattered bunches of cattle, antelope were never far distant. For meat we depended on the antelope, as it is better than elk or deer, but occasionally someone would kill a deer or an elk for a change; these animals were on either side of the valley in considerable numbers. On the night Jim and I reached camp, the other boys were talking of one antelope which all had been trying to kill ever since they had come into the valley. This animal had one regular prong, but the other was deformed so that it resembled a bull's horn somewhat. It was my luck on the next day to kill that antelope, and I still have his head, which is the largest I have ever seen. The same day on the northerly side of the river Charley Metzel killed the largest blacktail deer any of us had ever seen. This deer had "antlers like a sage brush." The head shows 19 prongs, and there are 38 points over an inch long. This trophy has been exhibited at the World's Fair (1893), the Louisiana Purchase Exposition (1904), at our State Fair, and elsewhere, always winning first prize.

Riding herd was not at all difficult. The only irksome part of the work was to stay in camp to keep a band of Indians in the valley from stealing everything, while the other boys were away. We had lots of fun, plenty of bad horses to ride (none of which I rode), and many thrilling exhibitions in the morning. We also had tremendous appetites. There were nine of us, and one evening Ben Hatfield with four others came in and camped nearby. We ate a hearty supper and went over to the Hatfield camp, distant probably a hundred feet, to spend that evening. After we had been there about an hour someone—it probably was Ben, though doubtless he will deny it—suggested that he was hungry. One of our boys said that the kid—referring to me—had killed a fat doe the day before, and he thought some of that would taste pretty good if roasted over the fire.

The suggestion met with unanimous approval. The doe, which was hanging from a quaking asp, was skinned, and parts of the loin were cut away, roased over the fire, and eaten. The flavor of the fire, with a little salt added, rendered the meat delicious. As the evening drew on, the eating continued until the carcass was stripped of meat. The group ate that entire antelope except the bones, after dinner!

When it came time to brand, Jim Williams and I, with the running gears of the wagon, hauled sufficient timber to build a large corral in which the nine of us branded between four and five hundred calves for the different owners. This task completed, I returned to the home range with the wagon, killing a fat antelope on the way.

The range did not look good in late September, 1886, although no one anticipated that the most disastrous winter in the history of cattle raising in Montana was about to ensue. During that winter, in parts of Montana, great herds of cattle were wiped out entirely.

It was in the early part of 1887 that Charley Russell sent the famous message to Stadler and Kaufman, his employers in Helena, "The Last of Five Thousand." The winter, which commenced early, was severe from the start; the snow was deep; and there was little chance for cattle upon the range. In our valley the fodder in the fields was soon exhausted, and the haystacks rapidly melted away.

When February 1st arrived, Captain Williams foresaw that unless there was a break in the weather, most of the cattle would starve to death. The upper fields were practically barren, and the cattle were placed in the lower field, which adjoins the Puller Springs property. He went there on foot, a distance of a mile and a half, every day to inspect the starving brutes, often continuing to the saloon at Puller Springs, where he sought to drown his sorrow. When he arrived at home, tired and discouraged and with liquor on his breath, his condition was not commented on with favor.

About the middle of the month he went to Virginia City, where he talked with Henry Elling, the banker, but there was no use in doing that. Hay was not to be bought even if the

"The Last of the 5000," by Charles M. Russell. *Courtesy of the Montana Historical Society and the Montana Stockgrowers' Association, Inc.*

firm's credit would have been deemed sufficient for an additional loan. Whether Captain Williams then had in his mind the idea of ending it all, no one will ever known, but he purchased an ounce bottle of laudanum. He returned to the ranch, where conditions were daily growing worse.

On February 20th, it started to snow heavily and continued the next day. On that day, the 21st, he went to the lower field, where the cattle were humped up with their heads to the ground, starving to death. The snow was falling heavily. He rounded a dense clump of willows, some four or five acres in extent, as if to inspect the 50 or 60 head of cattle which were assembled between the willows and the fence, then turned abruptly and walked about 150 yards towards Puller Springs; he then backtracked carefully to the willows; probably he hoped the snow would cover his tracks. How he managed to penetrate the thick willow copse for 60 or 75 feet no one ever knew. He did not return home that night or the next day. Late in the afternoon of the second day the boys went to the "Springs" to bring him home, but he was not there. The alarm was spread, and an intensive search was begun, all the neighbors joining in. But he could not be found.

Finally someone, who availed himself of his knowledge of hunting, followed the tracks from the willows toward Puller Springs and, when he reached their end, concluded that the person who made them had backtracked. Eventually the snow-covered body of the Captain was found in the thick willows. He had taken off his mittens, drunk the laudanum, pulled his cap over his eyes, and gone to sleep.

He was buried in the graveyard on the point of benchland which looks down upon the Ruby, as it turns from west to north at the great bend, and for many years he lay in an unmarked grave. That did not matter much; the good he did was not interred with his bones.

Apparently, however, James Williams had won the oblivion he sought. Men seemingly forgot him, and forgot who it was that as executive officer of the Vigilantes had rendered such signal service.

Twelve years passed. In August of 1899 the State Association of Montana Pioneers met in Virginia City, the largest meeting the association ever held; men and women came from far and near, even from distant states, to renew the memories of youth and to meet the friends of yesteryear. There was, of course, much talk of the Vigilantes, of the leaders of that sterling band, of the road agents, of Slade and Maria Virginia

Henry Elling, Banker.

Virginia City, M. T. 2/23 188 7

Jn. E. Callaway Esq
Butte Mont

Dear Sir:
        Joseph T. Haines
has just came in from
Hoser Park, and reports
Capt James Williams dead,
supposed to have committed
suicide by taking laudanum

                Yours truly
                Henry Elling

Reproduction of note from banker Henry Elling to Colonel James Edmund Callaway telling of the suicide of Captain James Williams. Courtesy of Montana Historical Society.

Slade, his wife. Here and there a group spoke of Captain Williams, but the mass had forgotten him. Was he to be forgotten altogether?

Shortly before the meeting adjourned, a writer, likening Williams to Cyrano de Bergerac, and employing as a prelude, "There was the allegory of my whole life: I, in the shadow at the ladder's foot, while others lightly mount to . . . fame," presented the essential facts in an article in the *Alder Gulch Times*, an ambitious upstart then bidding for a place in the newspaper field, concluding with this sentence, "And not until he is accredited his proper place in the history of this State will its history be properly written, or posterity's debt to his memory be paid."

The article received widespread attention, and a somewhat intensive discussion ensued, oral as well as written. Upon investigation, no one was found who denied, nor could anyone upon the facts deny, that James Williams was the executive officer, the leader of the Vigilantes in the field. Official recognition came in 1907 through the enactment by the Tenth Legislative Assembly of House Bill No. 49, appropriating $250 "to purchase a bronze tablet to the memory of Captain James Williams, and to pay for its erection in the main hall of the Capitol."

The credit for this emplacement belongs chiefly to the Hon. Frank B. Linderman, LL.D., author of *Indian Why Stories, American,* and other well-known books. Mr. Linderman was then a resident of Madison County, having represented that county in the lower house of the legislative assembly in 1903. In 1907 he was deputy secretary of state; he drew the bill, had it introduced, and when it received the governor's signature filed it in the office of the secretary of state. As acting secretary of state, his chief, Secretary of State Yoder, being absent on account of illness, he wrote the inscription and otherwise carried into effect the legislative will. The tablet bears this inscription:

To commemorate the name and deeds of James Williams, captain of the Vigilantes, through whose untiring efforts and intrepid daring, law and order were established in Montana, and who, with his associates, brought to justice the most desperate criminals in the Northwest.

Some years later a member of the family placed a modest granite stone over the mounds which marked the resting places of James and Elizabeth Ledford Williams.

Appendices

Gold Rush to Moran Creek, 1898

ALMOST as early as I can remember, prospectors were hunting for gold and going to places where it was reported there had been a "strike." One would see a prospector, sometimes several prospectors, getting ready to go—fitting a buck board, a wagon, or packing horses or burros. I remember well the continuous string of prospectors who set out to join the stampede to the Black Hills. They went by twos or threes, sometimes one alone. The pack animal, or vehicle, would carry bedding, cooking utensils, and the like. On top of the pack would appear the inevitable pick and shovel, usually a gold pan. All were armed to fight off Indians. The prospector took his rifle on his saddle horse or carried it if afoot. Besides the rifle he usually strapped around his waist a cartridge belt to which was hung a six-shooter and a knife.

There were local prospectors on the go not far from Virginia City all the time, except in dead winter. One of these was a man named Hathaway who maintained a wife, an excellent woman, at a home up Alder Gulch. Hathaway had four burros which he took upon lengthy expeditions into the hills.

I had heard of mining stampedes in which an entire camp would rush forth in a kind of frenzy. Such were the stampedes from Bannack to Alder Gulch and the Salmon River stampede, in which many lost their lives.

But on July 28, 1898, long after the historic stampedes, something happened in Virginia City. Living there at the time was Benjamin J. Fine, a mining man, who had cut a large figure in the operation of the Easton mine in Brown's Gulch. Some smart-aleck had attempted to "job" Fine without success.

Shortly after this Fine left Virginia City one morning in a buggy drawn by two horses. He took pains to apprise the jobber that he was going somewhere. He was plumb mysterious, as the cowboys say. Later in the day he returned to town, stopping at the house of a well known colored resident, Mrs. Bickford, who lived in Daylight Creek on the easterly way into the city. Mrs. Bickford, known to old residents as Sally, but at that time as the "water queen," as she owned the water works supplying the town, had been married to a white man who had placer mined on the West Fork of the Madison; and she had some gold dust. Mr. Fine, cautioning her to keep still, borrowed about a half ounce of dust, promising to return it, which he did.

Driving into town he alighted at the Madison House, finding the "jobber" in the bar room, as he had anticipated. There were perhaps a dozen men there. Fine came with a beaming face and invited all to have something. All responded. As they were lined up at the bar and about to drink, Fine took from his vest pocket a package which he opened mysteriously, showing the gold dust. It was coarse dust of good quality. Being asked where he got it, Fine refused to tell, but remarked that it was a pretty good morning's work. The excitement was intense. Why, a discovery of that kind reminded one of Alder Gulch or Last Chance or Confederate in the palmy days!

Mr. Fine's driver, perhaps by design, would say nothing except that he and Mr. Fine had been to Moran Creek. This creek is the outlet of Axolotl Lake. The creek runs precipitously for a short distance and then placidly to the farms below in the Madison Valley. The flow is small. As the word got about that Fine had been to Moran Creek and had a half ounce of fine gold dust, it was easy to put two and two together. The excitement of the bar room extended to the town and the stampede started. I never saw anything like it. Everyone who had a saddle horse hit out for Moran Creek. In a short time every horse in town had left, except a team which I had reserved to take my mother to the train at Twin Bridges, as she had planned a visit to my cousin, Mrs. Brantly, at Deerlodge.

A farmer had come to town with a team which was hitched to a post; some fellow unhitched the horses and took one of them, harness and all, and rode pell mell through town and across the hills. W. A. Clark was working in his law office when the news reached him. He ran across town to his stable, hurriedly saddled his horse, and, paying no attention to roads, hastened toward Three Mile Creek, which was on the way to Moran, losing his saddle blanket before he was out a mile. Tom Farrell, famous auctioneer in the early days, former sheriff, and noted horseman, knew one had to have water to placer mine and at once posted a notice on Moran Creek, claiming the water. People were arriving at Moran Creek with picks and shovels and with nothing. When the horses were gone, people left Virginia City on foot. Women went in considerable numbers, some afoot.

Some people took provisions, but most did not. The town was deserted. Of course, some remained who couldn't get away. A few were in on the secret. Jim Williams had come to town from the Upper Ruby and was there during the height of the excitement. He came to my office and told me to pay no attention to it; there was a "hoax somewhere." "I saw that gold," he said, "and it is West Fork gold. I know West Fork gold when I see it; you see Fine." I did so. Mr. Fine and I were good friends. He told me the truth saying he had no intention to stir up all of this; it got away from him; he simply wanted to fool this man who had attempted to job him; but he pledged me to secrecy.

Having occasion to go to the courthouse, I saw three young fellows on horses in Broadway Street near the county clerk's office. Going into that office, I perceived Henry Steffens, my intimate friend, writing out placer location notices. I said, "Henry, you aren't falling for this foolishness, are you? The idea that if there is any gold in Moran Creek those early day prospectors wouldn't have found it!" My approach wasn't good. Henry snapped, "There's a lot those old prospectors didn't know!" In a few moments the three men were on their way to the New Eldorado. It was about six miles from Virginia City to Moran Creek. The little creek was alive with fortune hunters. Notices of location were everywhere. The people talked excitedly. Soon they realized they were hungry, and, except in rare instances, none had anything to eat. Some stayed out late into the night and the night grew cold. My memory is that a few were out all night, suffering somewhat. During the day of July 28, 1898, Tom Thexton, who used the Moran Creek water for farming, heard of the excitement. Mounting a spirited horse he rode to the point at which most of the people were observing that Tom Farrell had posted a notice appropriating the water. His anger blazed. He did not like Farrell, and Farrell did not like him. Finding Farrell, he dismounted, and, during the altercation with him, hit Farrell over the head with a shovel, knocking him to the ground. Tom got on his horse and attempted to ride the horse upon the body of his prostrate enemy, so witnesses said, but Tom denied that. Anyhow, Miss Grace McStay of Waterloo, Iowa, who was visiting her sister Mrs. W. W. Cheely, wife of the editor of the *Madisonian*, was present at the altercation. She grabbed the bridle-bit and, standing over the prostrate form of Mr. Farrell, held the horse back. Miss McStay was acclaimed a heroine and her exploit was printed in eastern papers. Mr. Farrell was brought to town for treatment and recovered.

In the meantime there was much discussion among those who remained in town. Along in the evening Fred F. Ellis, a dentist, who had an interest in a claim located by a small group, told me and some others in front of the post office, which was then across the street from the Madison House, that he wouldn't take a million dollars for his rights. Being in the know, I scoffed at him. Of course, there was no gold in Moran Creek. In a short time the stampede was not even referred to.

But as an aftermath Tom Thexton was arrested for his assault on Tom Farrell. When the trial came on, I represented the State. Thexton was found guilty, sentenced to six months in jail and fined $500.00.

The Story of George Ives

By Colonel Wilbur Fisk Sanders [1]

ON THE 18TH day of December I was at Nevada City, having a final interview with a gentleman who had taken an interest in endeavoring to secure the creation and organization of a new territory in eastern Idaho, and was about to return to Virginia City, whence the next morning I was to go to Bannack, my home, and where I anticipated spending my first Christmas in the mountains, when my attention was attracted to a cavalcade of horsemen coming up the main street. As they approached I recognized them as the gentlemen who had gone down the Gulch the day before to detect and arrest, if possible, Tbolt's murderers, with four or five additional persons.

Twilight had already come, and they stopped without dismounting in the middle of the road and continued a discussion as to whether they would take the prisoners to Virginia City, or remain with them at Nevada. From the trend of their observations it was apparent this had been the subject of some previous consideration. There were those who thought it was due to the prisoners that they should have the selection of the forum for their trial, and Ives expressed an ear-

---

[1] Reprinted with permission from Helen Fitzgerald Sanders and William H. Bertsche, Jr., *X. Beidler: Vigilante* (Norman: University of Oklahoma Press, 1957), pp. 51–79.

nest desire to be conducted to Virginia City, where he said he had "friends." Others were of the opinion that deference to established custom required that the prisoners, without regard to the mere desire of any one of them should be tried by some substantial tribunal nearest the scene of the tragedy,—a vague recognition of the value of the Anglo-Saxon doctrine of the jury of the vicinage. Upon putting the question to the vote the prisoners and Jimmy Gibbings assumed to vote, and the question seemed to be in danger of becoming a tie, when someone insisted that it was a question upon which none should vote but those who had made the arrest, and had charge of the prisoners, and so it was determined that they should be tried in Nevada mining district, which was nearest to Ives' ranch, with the insignificant exception of Junction Mining District, then in a chrysalis and fickle state, having been recently organized. The prisoners were taken to a small warehouse on the main street which seemed to offer reasonable security and accommodation, their blankets and robes given them, a guard appointed, and the crowd dispersed.

On my way up to Virginia City, I met a lawyer of prominence and ability hastening down to Nevada, who advised me that some of his clients were in trouble, having been accused and arrested for the murder of the "Dutchman." He said he was counsel for "these fellows," whoever he may have meant thereby. This lawyer was James M. Thurmond, who asked me to return with him, stating there was an opportunity for me to make a good fee, as they had plenty of money. I proceeded towards Virginia City, and shortly met another lawyer, John D. Ritchie, one of the earliest practitioners in this region, who was considered essential to the winning of cases, whether before mining judges, or juries on miners' meetings. He was already far gone with consumption, against which he made a stout fight for a number of years, finally dying at Missoula.

Arriving at the foot of Wallace Street in Virginia City, I saw Harry Percival Adams Smith, another lawyer, who, though somewhat demoralized, was a man of very remarkable ability. He was fortifying himself at the last place of entertainment, for his journey to Nevada, and advised me that he had been sent for to help some of "the boys" out of a scrape. These three lawyers were somewhat remarkable characters, all of them out to thwart the administration of justice by all the means they could invent.

The next morning, in the store of D. W. Tilton & Co., where A. J. Oliver & Co. kept their express office, which assumed largely the business of a stage and postoffice, I was purchasing my ticket for a passage to Bannack, when I was accosted by A. J. Culbertson, with the statement that the Lott Brothers wished to see me at once at Nevada. I told him I was going through Nevada on the stage in the course of a couple of hours, and would take occasion to see them as I passed through. He stated to me, however, that there was much urgency in their desire, and that he thought I should go to them at once without waiting for the coach or purchasing my ticket, and I accompanied him forthwith to Nevada.

Arriving there I was advised by these gentlemen that the lawyers then practicing in Alder Gulch had all been engaged, so far as they could ascertain, to defend the murderers of Tbolt; that the testimony which had been secured demonstrated that the guilty parties had been arrested; that it had been a most cruel murder, and they greatly desired that I should remain to prosecute the defendants. I had not been present at any trial for homicide in the mountain region, but my ears had been filled with stories of the provoking miscarriages of justice with a single exception, arising largely from the disinclination of participants to accept the responsibilities which their position imposed. The courts would disclaim responsibility as to the facts of any murder, and lawyers would tell the jury that if the defendant was guilty he should be convicted, but if they entertained a reasonable doubt he should be acquitted; that the jurymen were the judges of the fact, and that they must do what they thought was right, etc. The lawyers disclaimed any inclination to argue upon one side or the other as to the guilt or innocence of the parties accused. Of course, the preliminary motions to quash the proceedings, to defer the trial, to continue the case, to delay the matter until the sense of offended justice had somewhat died out of the community; till opportunity had been afforded to ascertain who were the witnesses; to scatter or manipulate them by such persuasions as they were susceptible to, were as well known then as now, and were practiced with unfailing uniformity. I had made up my mind in the light of all this history and from my knowledge of human nature, as it appeared in the administration of criminal law, that if I should prosecute any case, I would push it with the utmost vigor, and if the guilt of the accused was certain, that the retribution should be swift, and absolutely remorseless. This was essential in defence of every person who took a responsible and active part in the prosecution, and it was a matter also of personal self-defence. The surroundings did not wholly prophesy the character of this prosecution, nor all that transpired, but I accepted the position.

Having gathered from the members of the *posse* the story of the killing of Tbolt, as they had ascertained it from John Frank and others, I interviewed him and Palmer, who had discovered the body, and found them apparently willing to testify. The citizens of Nevada and miners from up and down the Gulch had assembled in considerable numbers before noon upon a mining claim between the Main Street of Nevada and Alder Creek, and I went there, practically an unknown person, to find a meeting presided over by Hon. Don L. Byam, and the lawyers and miners considering the code of criminal procedure to be observed in the trial of this particular case. In the absence of the defendants, their lawyers were desirous that the trial should be in the regular form, before a miner's judge and a jury of six or twelve men selected in the usual way, but it had already been voted that the trial should take place before the miners of the Gulch en masse, to be presided over by Judge Byam, with the assistance of the judge of Junction Mining District below Nevada, who fulfilled the office of *puisne* judge, and a motion was made that lawyers should not be permitted to participate in the trial. This question begot a heated discussion, in which Messrs. Thurmond, Ritchie, and Smith took an important part, and with Col. J. M. Wood, and some other citizens, advocating the right of the parties to be represented by counsel. The proposition, however, was vehemently, if not stoutly, opposed by a great many orators present from the sluice-boxes and the unfortunate lawyers suffered much depreciation, and excoriation. The discussion lasted for an hour or more, and one of the participants, most loud-mouthed and censorious in his denunciation of the profession, was the owner of a mine at the mouth of Brown's Gulch, who had recently belonged to a Detroit regiment in the Federal army, and who upon this occasion wore his uniform. It may seem laughable or even trifling, but watching the drift and current of speech on that occasion, I do not doubt but that his uniform lost him his case.

After the discussion had been unduly prolonged, someone suggested that they would like to hear my opinion as to the advisability of permitting lawyers to participate, and in response to the invitation I mounted the wagon, and looked out upon the somewhat heterogeneous crowd, with a few exceptions being to me entire strangers. I was conscious that I was subjected to a somewhat inquisitive inspection, for the lawyers who represented the defendants to that moment were the leaders of the Bar, and represented its intellect and influence in the various controversies appealing to courts and masses for determination. There had been added that morning to the trio I have already mentioned, Alexander Davis, Esq., a most excellent and pertinacious gentleman, who was a substantial addition in more ways than one to the defendant's strength.

There were, indeed, three or four other lawyers in the Gulch, who subsequently practised their profession, but they had not yet assumed to practice law there, or were such recent arrivals as that their capacity had not become known. I did not think it desirable to appear as taking a great interest in the question of permitting counsel, although my own conviction was, that if the defendants desired lawyers to defend them it should, under all circumstances, be granted. I said to the crowd that in determining a question of that character they should have regard to the final result, that if the parties should be tried and convicted or acquitted, whether they would be more satisfied with the result according as they had granted or refused them the privilege of being heard by counsel, and that I thought

198

they should consider the matter seriously in that light. I mentioned casually that I had been spoken to by friends of the party who had been killed to prosecute the case, if the lawyers were permitted to participate, and that I trusted we should be able in that case to come at the truth of the matter, and protect all the interests confided to our care.

The crowd looked at me curiously as if taking the measure of my abilty to cope with the great lawyers of established reputation who were on the other side, and they did not give any sign of satisfaction with the condition. However, on putting the question to the vote, our ex-federal soldier was beaten, and it was determined that the defendants should have the benefit of counsel, if benefit it were.

It was late in December, and the weather was somewhat cold. It was very evident that the men who were to try the defendants, would not, all of them, hear all the testimony, and therefore upon my motion it was resolved that they should be separately tried, and that as to Ives, who was universally recognized as the principal culprit, we should have from each of the mining districts twelve jurymen, making twenty-four in all, whose duty it should be to listen to all the proof, and give such advice to the meeting as justly resulted therefrom. Whereupon Judge Byam wrote the names of twelve miners, Judge Wilson the names of twelve others, and it was moved that these twenty-four should constitute the jurors in the case whose duties were advisory merely.

The excitement of the crowd meanwhile had greatly increased. From eight to ten miles up the gulch, and two to three miles below, the miners, with their guns, were arriving in great numbers, until a thousand or fifteen hundred had assembled around that wagon. At this stage of the proceedings Mr. J. B. Cavan, a bailiff or deputy sheriff of Henry Plummer's, mounted the wagon and read a list of twelve names of citizens of Fairweather Mining District, whom he moved should be added to the twenty-four already selected. I thought the jury somewhat clumsy by reason of its number, and I objected to adding the list of Mr. Cavan thereto, saying that it appertained to the organized mining districts with a chosen judicial autonomy to try the defendants, which were nearest the scene of the crime; that we had included Nevada mining dstrict by reason of the incompleteness and smallness of the organization at Junction, and that I did not think it wise to enlarge it by going yet further up the Gulch, and that no reason could be given, if we did proceed further, why Highland Mining District, and Pine Grove, and Summit might not also claim the privilege of increasing the number of the jury.

The deliberations of the forenoon, and the vote upon the proposition to allow Ives the privilege of counsel, not only gave confidence to the lawyers, but it emboldened his chums, allies, and sympathizers in the crowd, who took a very active part in the proceedings, and in the applause, which became somewhat frequent, and it was apparent that a fight was on of very great strenuousness. The "good fellows," the popular fellows, the generous fellows, the well-known fellows, in short, the boys, without care or knowledge of Ives' guilt or innocence, led by a half-dozen active colleagues of Ives, had interested themselves in the controversy, and made that interest manifest by encouragement or interruptions with great freedom. When I had finished what I had to say against adding to the twenty-four jurors another list of twelve from the district above, Mr. Cavan vehemently shook a paper containing this list of names in my face, and before the assembled miners said, "Perhaps you have something to say against the character of these men I have named." As a matter of fact I did not know one of them, but as he had read the list I recognized the name of a prominent gambler at Virginia City, with whom I subsequently became acquainted, and feeling bound to maintain the rights of the prosecution there, I replied that I had nothing to say against the list of names, that I did not know one of them, and that if what I heard with reference to some of them was true, I had no desire to make their acquaintance. This excited his anger to a somewhat intemperate degree, and standing by my side, speaking to me for the benefit of the crowd, he said, "I will hold you personally responsible for that remark,"—and the whole tumult of the Ives' trial arose that moment. In that strange and new country it would not do to treat a remark of that kind with indifference, nor the speaker without some personal attention, and in language as pregnant with meaning as I could select, I gave him a verbal castigation in the presence of that crowd which permitted no misunderstanding as to its significance. I said I was busy in a matter which occupied my time, that I did not fail to apprehend the meaning of his remark when used by gentlemen, that evidently he had indulged in that speech to advertise a courage which he did not possess, that I was reasonably certain that he was a coward, but that at the close of the trial I should be in the vicinity, and could be found. This little colloquy stirred the miners profoundly, and by their cheers they seemed to think he got no more than he deserved, and they looked at me with increasing interest, and apparent confidence.

I think it just to Mr. Cavan to say that a subsequent acquaintance with him, and a knowledge of his career for some years thereafter dissipated any supposition that his action resulted from any sympathy with highway robbery and murder, or any desire to shield and protect the guilty, but that it was a move by him which he thought would be popular and make him friends.

It was now noon, and Judge Byam declared the meeting adjourned till after dinner. Robert Hereford was Judge Byam's executive officer in his position as sheriff of Nevada Mining District, and Adriel B. Davis the sheriff of Junction Mining District acted as Hereford's deputy. At this time Judge Wilson approached me, and inquired if I desired assistance in the prosecution, and oppressed somewhat with the growing consequence of the battle, I cheerfully said I did. He said there was a lawyer who was mining at Junction, who he thought could render valuable help, and I asked him to introduce me to him. He brought to me a short, stubby, hairy, fatherly-looking man, somewhat rude, of dilapidated garb, whose bootlegs did not have sufficient fibre to stand up, and into one of which he had vainly essayed to tuck one of the legs of his pantaloons. He spoke intelligently, and made it manifest that his indignation was deeply stirred by the events which had transpired, and I counted it fortunate that on all accounts such a find had been made. His name was Charles S. Bagg, and I found no occasion to regret his identification with the prosecution.

If the lawyers for the defence appealed to the miners on questions submitted, the appeal of my colleague was with greater frequency and intensity to the Almighty, with whom, judging from his speech, he was on terms of considerable intimacy. He lacked nothing of audacity and volubility, and being himself a miner, he appealed to the assemblage on their level with great effect, his courage was equal to the duty, and he rendered good service throughout the trial.

After dinner the scene of the event was changed from the mining claim where the morning session had been held to the east side of the main street in Nevada, where a big Schuttler wagon had been drawn up in front of a two story building, some seats arranged for the Court, counsel, and prisoners in the same, and a fire had been built on the ground near the wagon from cord wood which some unlucky woodman had the misfortune to have placed in that vicinity. William Y. Pemberton, Esq., then a genial young lawyer living at Virginia City, was appointed amanuensis and a table was provided for him near the fire. A semi-circle of benches from an adjacent hurdy-gurdy house had been placed round the fire for the accommodation of the twenty-four jurors, and behind that semi-circle a place was reserved for a cordon of guards, who with their shotguns or rifles as the case might be, marched hour by hour. Beyond them, and round on their flank stood a thousand or fifteen hundred miners, teamsters, mechanics, merchants, gamblers, all sorts and conditions of men, deeply interested in the proceedings. As a rule, it was a good-natured crowd and not unduly boisterous, and all had the right of participating in the discussions and other proceedings if they chose, of which quite a number from time to time availed themselves. There was frequent objection to the relevancy or pertinency of proposed proof, and whenever a proposition was submitted to a vote, the absent participants were summoned from the restaurants, saloons, stores, barber shops, and other places of resort to give their vote upon the objections, which was generally without merit, and were overruled.

While it was cold, there was very little suffering, and during the middle part of the day the sun, which swung lazily round the southern horizon, gave some warmth. The miners were generally warmly dressed, and did not make any complaints, nor abandon in the least degree the purpose for which they had come to trial. Another freight wagon with a very high seat had been conveniently placed for the accommodation of the witness who was testifying, in view of all the persons present. The first witness was Palmer, who, mounting the high seat above the entire crowd presented a somewhat uncouth appearance, as with bared head, and long hair hanging upon his shoulders, he told the story of his acquaintance with Ives, his finding of the dead body, his application for assistance in loading it into his wagon, and the declination thereof. This story he told in a loud and confident voice with perfect freedom, and apparent willingness, and his manner seemed to give confidence to the subsequent witnesses. Expectation stood on tip-toe as to what the proof would be, for rumor asserted that some one had turned State's evidence, if that is a name to apply where it was a thousand miles to a State.

From the opening of the trial new facts began to come to the ears of the prosecution, told generally in whispers, with a request that the name of the person imparting the information might be withheld, or in some instances that it might be made to appear that the information was compulsorily extorted. The afternoon of the 19th of December saw the trial fairly under way. The miners adjourned till 9 o'clock the next morning, and the prisoners were remanded to the warehouse under guard.

There was no lull in the excitement, while rumors came from every point of the compass, prophesying dire disaster to the prosecution or defence, according to the inclination of the prophet or liar who invented them. Detectives and pickets were detailed to watch events during the preliminary proceedings, and for the first day or two of the trial "Alec" Carter and "Doc" Hunter, with a half dozen other friends of Ives who were believed to be identified with him in his crimes, had been very active in his behalf, insisting upon whatever, in their judgment, would insure his acquittal. Plummer, the acknowledged civic magnate of that Gulch and the entire country, and the elected sheriff, under the mining regulations of two districts remote from each other, was a name to conjure with an object of great interest, and rumor affirmed that he was on his way from Bannack to take the prisoners from the possession of the party who had them in charge and on trial. As a matter of actual fact, when the prisoners had been brought to Nevada, by the advice of their counsel George Lane, brutally nicknamed "Club-foot George," had been dispatched in the night to Bannack for Plummer's presence and assistance. But there were rumors circulating in Bannack which disturbed the confidence of Plummer and illustrated that "uneasy lies the head that wears a crown." It was said there that there had been formed in Alder Gulch a great vigilance committee intent on ridding the country of the lawful authorities, and divers and sundry good citizens besides, whose names were given with a view to add to the obloquy of such a movement. These rumors found credence with Plummer, and with other good citizens of Bannack, and a picket post was established on the top of the mountain divide, between the Grasshopper and Rattlesnake, to watch the approach of such a party so all the importunings of Plummer to go to the rescue were declined.

Ives was primarily accused and tried for murder, and in tracing his whereabouts for the summer and fall preceding, circumstances of robbery and murder thickened around him, and the names of his companions on these forays were blurted out by witnesses with a brutal frankness, and the testimony assumed a wider scope than the mere proof of killing Tbolt. As the names of these active participants, in the earlier portion of the proceedings were frequently repeated, under circumstances showing their identification with Ives' crimes, a prudent regard for their own safety silenced them, and retiring to the rear of the trial some of them disappeared. Of course, such an assemblage was a motley crowd, made up as it was of all classes of people inhabiting the Gulch. Generally it may be said they were sober, industrious, adventurous, hard-working miners, with a clear conception of their right to be, to do, to have and to keep; with a strong sense of justice, born, not of studying the definition in the books, but of that experience derivable from contact with the world and its affairs. Merchants and freighters, mechanics and teamster, equally sober and impelled by like convictions, constituted a limited fraction of the crowd.

One of the active partipants in the discussion was a man from Georgia, Col. John M. Wood, who divided his time between mining, speculating, carousing and preaching the Gospel to congregations yet ruder than he. His motive in mingling actively in this trial was probably a desire to introduce himself to the community and establish his character as a man of some consequence, for with all his activity it is not probable that he had any sympathy with the crimes then frequent. He had come from Colorado, and what though he clung to his Baptist religion with great vigor, he had a wild latitudinarianism which rendered it very uncertain on which side of any controversy impinging on morals he would be found. In the various discussions in which he took part, he was uniformly found, for reasons which he plausibly dressed, on the side of the culprits, until the crowd, which through all the proceedings maintained an imperturbable good nature, occasionally jeered him. I am sorry I cannot name all of the miners and others who participated in these discussions, which prolonged the trial unnecessarily, but it was thought advisable to give the amplest latitude to discussion, and an equal freedom to decision.

The testimony of John Frank, given freely and with apparent candor, told the circumstances of the killing of Tbolt. Tbolt had appeared at Ives' ranch or headquarters, presented the order of Mr. Clark for the mules, and they had been brought up and delivered to him. They were large, and very valuable, and feeding on the nutritious grass had become silky and high-spirited. When Tbolt came to settle the bill, his buckskin purse, out of which the dust was weighed, contained three or four hundred dollars. Mounting one of the mules, he started across the valley toward the highway leading to Alder Gulch. After he had departed Ives suggested that it was a pity to let all that money go and the mules also, and when, by the toss of a gold coin, the lot fell to him to prevent it, he saddled his horse, examined his revolver, and galloped after his victim. Returning with the mules in a short time, in a spirit of explanation or bravado, he said that it seemed cowardly to shoot a fellow in the back, and when he approached near enough, he holloaed, and when Tbolt turned round, he made a centre shot, hitting him in the head. He took the purse, and drove the mules back to camp.

The stage drivers upon the line from Virginia City and Bannack, regular and occasional, gave much information as to Ives' connection with robberies and murders occurring along that highway, and of persons who were cognizant of the same, but it was thought prudent to excuse them from testifying, because of their necessary exposure to the vengeance of Ives and his partners in crime, but the proof of the killing of Tbolt, of the fact that Ives had been engaged in coach robberies, had perpetrated other murders, and had spent weeks along the line of exit out of the country where treasure was carried was ample and absolutely conclusive. The foolish attempt by some of his partners in crime to establish an alibi as to some of these crimes broke down ignominiously, and it became very apparent to his counsel on the second day of the trial that if he were to be acquitted or otherwise escape, it must be for something other than the result of the proof, and with great ingenuity they sought to bring the prosecution into contempt, and excite the prejudices of the crowd against it. Long John, who had turned State's evidence, and related the circumstances of the main tragedy with great distinctness, and who had been corroborated by many circumstances relevant and irrelevant, came in for the seven vials of the lawyer's wrath. They dwelt, with great fervor and indignation upon the infamy manifested by a participant in crime who would "peach on his pals," and argued that whatever might be said as to the actual perpetrator of the crime, the traitor should never be permitted to escape. A code of morals sounding very much like this re-appeared in Montana a generation later. Before Ives' case was disposed of, his several lawyers seemed to think they had firmly established the proposition that whatever was the result as to Ives, Long John should certainly be executed.

The great excitement culminated upon the last day of the trial which was almost wholly devoted to the arguments of the case. The proximity of two hostile armies would not have been more productive of wild, contradictory, and misleading rumors than were the circumstances of this investigation. The air was filled with all manner of tragic and absurd reports of what was doing and being done and going to be done elsewhere pertaining to the trial, but the crowd hung to the investigation with a tightening grip which no exciting tale of possible discomfiture could in the least degree relax, and on the morning of 21st of December the case opened with as large an attendance, and as firm a purpose as existed when it began. During arguments upon the admissibility of testimony many of the facts had been discussed, and the final arguments of the case were threshing over old straw. In these preliminary arguments Messrs. Davis and Smith had largely engaged, being gentlemen of ingenious talents and great plausibility of speech, and Messrs. Ritchie and Thurmond had somewhat reserved their efforts for the final arguments. If the rumors contemporaneous with the introduction of proof augmented the excitement to fever heat, the arguments of counsel added fuel to the flame. I cannot think that the testimony introduced to that assemblage left a particle of doubt in the mind of any spectator of the following five facts:

1st. That Ives killed Tbolt as charged.

2nd. That he had committed a half dozen other murders in the vicinity of equal cruelty.

3rd. That he was the leading actor in robbing the stage passengers between Rattlesnake Ranch and Bannack in October, when Dan McFadden, Leroy Southmayd, and others were passengers.

4th. That he had pursued the vocation of a highway robber for number of months along the roads leading to Salt Lake City.

5th. That he belonged to the Criminal classes, and that his appetite for blood had grown till it became a consuming passion.

Ives' demeanor during the trial was quiet, and without apparent anxiety; he did not prejudice his case by any unmannerly demonstration, contrasting in this repect somewhat with his counsel, who at times seriously tried the patience of their auditors. The opening argument was by Mr. Bagg, and was a strong appeal to the citizens who had isolated themselves, and endured the hardships of mining and mining life to better their condition, now that they had certainly found one of the free-booters who infested the highways to make of him an example to all persons in like manner offending.

When the arguments opened I sent a note to Mr. John A. Creighton, a popular merchant at Virginia City, a king among the pioneers, telling him that the crisis had finally arrived, and asking him to bring with him all the good men he could find, and remain till the end.

The people of the West are very susceptible to the influence of speech, possibly not discriminating very closely as to its proprieties, and statements that an able speaker will occupy a given rostrum will attract more hearers in the West than elsewhere, and in that early day without newspapers or magazines or frequent occasions for oratory, such a symposium as was there promised attracted nearly every person in the Gulch to Nevada. The counsel for Ives were unquestionably discouraged with the strength of the case for the prosecution, at the poverty of their own resources for the defence and some humiliating exposures of the invalidity of the defence which they set up, and some of them indulged in libations much beyond what prudence would have dictated, though none but Mr. Ritchie seemed to have impaired their keenness of intellect by such indulgence. The hindrances during the progress of the trial seriously tried the patience of the miners, who were eager to return to the claims which they were opening to take advantage of the first rush of waters, and they interrupted counsel for the defence frequently by cat-calls and other signs of disapproval, feeling that their good nature and generosity were being imposed on, as indeed, in instances, was unquestionably true. I found frequent occasions to importune the crowd, whatever they felt was the provocation, to give them the amplest opportunity to say everything which they desired; an appeal which was, in every instance, I believe, successful. Occasionally there would burst from the throat of some witty spectator a remark which would set the crowd laughing, and sometimes a labored argument of a lawyer would be exploded by a common sense observation from some hard headed miner in the audience, who would wipe the labored structure of counsel off the boards in five words.

There was no bad temper in the crowd, except as to some of Ives' friends, but rather a stern purpose to see that complete justice was done, whatever and whoever stood in the way, and the passion grew as the speeches continued, and the hours waned.

Mr. Ritchie followed with an argument for his client, as good probably as could be made, but which did not, in my estimation, call for any special remark. He appealed to the softer side of human nature and clearly demonstrated that Tbolt could not be brought back to life, that everybody knew Ives was a clever fellow, generous and a little wild, and no one could tell what were the exact circumstances under which Tbolt was killed. Ives himself did not testify. Mr. Thurmond followed Mr. Ritchie, who, having become physically exhausted, repaired to some neighboring place of entertainment where liquid delights, as they are misnamed, were dispensed, and having somewhat over-estimated his capacity in that regard, during the balance of the arguments sat around muttering his discontent at the "outrages" which he saw in progress before him.

Thurmond was in many ways a masterful character; if a little coarse, he was strong in intellect. He had considerable pride to bring himself into the good opinion of those who met him, and his views generally agreed with, if they did not take their shape from the prevailing influences about him. His plea for Ives was able but it fell upon dull ears. A hundred or two men who would have been glad to see Ives acquitted more as a proof of their good-nature than otherwise, and the few who had been his companions in crime, at this stage of the proceedings constituted the outer portion of the crowd, whereas two days before they had been in its forefront.

The sun sent down about the closing of the arguments, the night air became more chilly, and those habituated to drink made more frequent visits to the saloons, of which there were a great number in the streets and alleys of the little hamlet. The fire was blazing brightly, and by the directions of the judge, the twenty-four jurymen retired to a neighboring store to consider what their report should be. The audience remained standing, as of course they had been during the three days of the trial, but they did not disperse.

Illustrative of the methods by which counsel for the defence sought to obtain sympathy for their client, and prejudice the prosecution, both Mr. Thurmond and Mr. Ritchie had referred to me as "the gentleman from Oberlin." In some cases that might have been of assistance, but in this particular case it did not do them any good. No one at the present time can fully appreciate the stigma, contumely, and obloquy in such an audience ordinarily attaching to the epithet "Oberlin." Of course, it was not a geographical location, but an intellectual, political, ethnological expression, designed to be a "crusher" when less Herculean methods had failed. It had occurred, much to my regret, that although living within forty miles of that historic town, and having some acquaintance with its professors and students, I had never been able to attend a Commencement of President Finney's famous college. Indeed, except to be whirled through Oberlin on a swiftly moving train, I had never been there, but I was disinclined to enter a plea of "not guilty" and amid the cheers of the assembled multitude, four-fifths of whom hated the name, Oberlin got a certificate of character, which, if it did not do her any good, extracted the virus from the railing accusations which had been made against the counsel for the prosecution.

It was apparent from the opening of the trial that law and order, or order without law, had locked horns with crime, and that it was to be a fight to a finish. All through the trial I had been considering what course should be pursued when it was made manifest that Ives was guilty, and he should be so declared, and I had resolved inexorably that instant, if I could influence events, he should be consigned to swift destruction. The blood of too many desperate characters was up, and it seemed due to everybody connected with the prosecution that a vengeance so swift and so stern should follow his conviction as to cause it to be known that henceforth peaceable people would be in possession of their own. I felt instinctively that the trial would culminate in a situation of much delicacy.

The twenty-four jurymen returned to their benches with a report in writing that Ives was guilty of the murder of Tbolt as charged, but I do not remember whether they took cognizance of his other offences or no, and this report was signed by twenty-three jurors only;

Henry Spivay declined to sign it not from any dissent, but for prudential reasons. The instant that report was read from the wagon, I made a motion, reciting that whereas George Ives for the murder of Nicholas Tbolt had been given a fair and impartial trial, with the privilege of being heard by council and witnesses, and had been reported to be guilty, that we approve of the verdict of the jury, and declare it to be the verdict of the miner's meeting, there assembled, and Judge Byam, without a moment's delay put my motion, and it was carried with a very loud shout, more than four-fifths of the citizens voting for the same. The significance of this movement did not seem to be appreciated by the defendant's counsel, and I instantly supplemented it with another motion, that George Ives, for the murder of which he was convicted, be now forthwith hung by the neck until he was dead. This motion being seconded, with equal promptness, Judge Byam put the motion and it was carried. It seems to me there was a feeble protest from Mr. Ritchie as to this last motion, to which it was replied that by the judgment of the meeting Ives had committed the murder, and punishment by hanging was the penalty. Whatever the facts were, there was no doubt as to the result, and Ives' friends, somewhat dazed by the swiftness with which these motions came, and the overwhelming support they received, turned their attention to an endeavor to have Long John hung at the same time.

Mr. Hereford and Mr. Davis were called to the wagon, and directed to carry the command of the meeting into immediate execution. Increasing the guard over Ives, who sat in a chair by the fire in front of the wagon, they went to find a suitable place to be used as a gallows. A cordon of pickets were stationed around the prisoner and the jury, all armed to the teeth, and the final event was awaited with profound expectancy the excitement momentarily increasing.

Ives finally arose from his seat, and came up into the wagon where I was standing. The excitement through the crowd was intense. A battle could scarcely have added anything to it. Ives came to me, and took me by the hand. If there was any tremor in his voice, or tremulousness in his person, I did not detect it, and the great crowd, always muttering something, was hushed into profound silence. For three days I had been expecting that this moment of exigency would arrive, and my mind was immovably made up as to what should be its outcome. Ives began by saying, "Colonel, I am a gentleman, and I believe you are, and I want to ask a favor which you alone can grant. If our places were changed, I know I would grant it to you, and I believe you will to me. I have been pretty wild away from home, but I have a mother and sisters in the States, and I want you to get this execution put off till tomorrow morning. I will give you my word and honor as a gentleman that I will not undertake to escape, nor permit my friends to try to change this matter."

I need not say that the appeal was one of great strength, but a simple event occurred, somewhat characteristic of the whole trial. One of the most noticeable, active and valuable men during its progress was a diminutive, short, young man acting as guard, vigilant, supple, observant, now here and now there wherever anything was to be done to secure the orderly conduct of the affair. He carried as did the majority of the crowd, a shotgun, the muzzle of which stood up a few inches above his head. He had gone from the crowd across the street, and climbed upon the dirt roof of a low log cabin where, from upon a ridgepole on the dirt, he was surveying from the rear the crowd surrounding the prisoner. Ives' request, spoken in an ordinary tone of voice, reached his ear, when he forthwith holloaed across the street, "Sanders, ask him how long a time he gave the Dutchman!," at which remark there was a ripple of laughter through the crowd, and while I had no thought to grant Ive's request and was reflecting in what manner of speech I should refuse it, and yet satisfy the sense of propriety of the miners, I have to confess that X. Beidler's remark lifted a considerable load from my mind. I replied to Ives, "You should have been thinking of this matter before. Get down there, maybe you can write a short letter to your folks before the sheriffs return for you. As to your property, I will make a motion which I think ought to satisfy you." He let go of my hand without response, jumped out of the wagon, sat down by the fire where some of his counsel were, and was furnished with a sheet of paper and a pencil, and proceeded to commence a letter to his mother.

Appendix B

I then moved that the Court take possesion of Ives' property and dispose of it, pay the board of the guard and the prisoner during the days of the trial, and remit whatever remained to Ives' mother, which motion was assailed by Mr. Ritchie in very denunciatory terms, he saying that it was an outrage to murder a man, and make him pay the board of those who had participated in it. This was met by some remarks from some of the crowd, largely by way of interruption, and as the trial was over, I responded to Mr. Ritchie's denunciation by saying that it was not unusual to tax the cost of a case to the defendant against whom judgment of death was entered, and that if a lawyer was not aware of that fact I thought he should go to a law school instead of a law office. The motion was carried, but my remark had stirred to a profounder depth than I had anticipated the anger of Lawyer Ritchie.

I had worn during the trial a heavy overcoat with deep side pockets, in each of which I had carried a new Colt's police pistol for a number of months. As the excitement culminated about the time the jury retired, at the closing of the arguments, it occurred to me that possibly they had been loaded so long that they might not readily respond if I wanted to use them, and I thought it best to ascertain their condition. I threw my coat aside, and with my hand on my revolver, I pulled the trigger, and it went off clear as a bell. The effect was exciting, for shooting scraps were matters of momentary expectancy, and a number of persons around me were startled; however, the ball entering the ground, did not further damage than leaving a hole in the lining of my coat. Its effect upon me was a strengthening of confidence. The opposing counsel during the trial had in instances engaged in bluffs and rebuffs, and as the culmination drew near in personal denunciation, and there were bad men on the confines of the crowd, capable of any crime which passion or recklessness could suggest. Every man participating in that prosecution took his life in his hand, and those more prominently identified with it were the objects of much contumely and resentment from the friends of the highway robbers. Mr. Ritchie came to the side of the wagon and pulling my overcoat and with some profane expletives said that he wanted to see me, that we would settle this matter then and there. I

213

alighted from the wagon, and he passed between two houses toward the rear, I following him, with an affair on my hands not pleasant nor wholly unexpected, but before we reached the rear of the houses, we were both seized by the sheriffs, or their assistants, and returned to the scene of the trial, where the excitement was unabated. Friends of Ives in considerable numbers were applying for permission to go inside the cordon of guards "to bid George Ives good-bye," and quite a number, some of them weeping bitterly, were granted the privilege.

Ives' effort to write a letter to his mother was interrupted by the excitement, and he did not finish it. In perhaps a half dozen lines of the fragment, he had written that he was surrounded by a mob who were going to hang him, and that he was seizing the few moments which remained of his life to write to her. If this was not the entire substance of what he wrote, it was practically the whole of it.

The sheriffs who had been gone for three-quarters of an hour, returned to report that they had been unable to find a convenient place to execute the orders of the miner's meeting, whereupon some-one said most any place would answer, and suggested that an un-finished log building adjoining the one in front of which the trial was held would answer as well as any other place, and mounting to the top of the logs, which were not covered by any roof, he threw down one end of the top log, and with assistance it was placed at an angle of about 45 degrees, so that the upper end of it protruded into the street. A rope was procured from an adjacent store, and tied around the end of the log; the sheriffs procured a dry goods box, and Ives was placed upon it under the dangling rope.

It has been generally stated that Ives pulled off his boots, saying he had sworn that he would not die with his boots on. I do not remem-ber this and only think it probable because it was told shortly there-after, and I cannot say that I ever contradicted it, which I should think I would have done had it not been true. However, I have not written the details of this prosecution, nor have I attempted to speak of it in detail, now for the first time putting down with pen the events as I remember them, without consultation with any other authorities whatever. In fact the written authorities of Langford and

Dimsdale are hearsay, neither one of these gentlemen having been present, but their information was gathered from actors in this stirring tragedy, and I consider them reliable. At least, where they differ from my own recollection, I find nothing inducing me to believe that there was any willful perversion of the facts.

As the denouement drew near the excitement increased, and the anger of Ives' friends mounted higher and higher, manifesting itself in much profane denunciation of the proceedings. A guard of probably one hundred men surrounded the box on which Ives stood, facing outward, and beyond them was a crowd of miners and citizens, undiminished in numbers. The sheriff placed the rope around Ives' neck, and he was asked by the judge if he wished to say anything. When this had been accomplished his friends apparently abandoned all hope of saving him, and made a rush toward the warehouse in which John Frank and Hillerman were confined, swearing that Long John should be hung at the same time, but that prison was surrounded by a guard as resolute and grim as was Ives himself, and their effort ended in signal failure and profuse profanity. Ives said only a few words, I remember he said that he was not guilty of this crime, and when he had apparently finished, the dry goods box was tumbled from under him, and his friends broke forth into vile exercrations toward those responsible for his taking off. The guard brought their guns down to the level, and there was a falling back of the crowd, but no dispersion of it, as it stood there for at least a half hour. The deed was done. Before there had been formal and perfunctory trials, amounting almost to challenges of the right of crime to rule in this region, but here there had been a strenuous controversy, a fair locking of horns between crime and order. It was yet to be determined, however, which should be master, for the disciples of disorder, discomfited, were by no means content to surrender to the reign of law. If not numerous, they were alert, active, defiant, and resourceful, and they did not intend to surrender at their first defeat. Many of them, intoxicated, breathed out threatenings and slaughter against prominent actors in the tragedy just closed, and they excited a wide apprehension that personal harm would come to me, and a guard of probably one hundred persons accompanied me to Virginia City, and in fact I was surrounded by a guard night and day for the week I remained in the Gulch.

The result of the trial among the miners, merchants, and other well disposed citizens was a subject of the profoundest congratulation. That evening I was in the store of Mr. John A. Creighton, with a number of gentlemen, conversing of the conditions surrounding the community, and listening to the turmoil of passion and hatred which seemed to have taken possession of the saloons, gambling houses, and dance houses along the street. Harvey Meade, a reputed desperado, who had escaped from the public justice of the Federal government at San Francisco, came into Mr. Creighton's wearing two revolvers in sight, and commenced an insolent conversation with me. It was said that he had been one of the conspirators to seize the revenue cutter *Chapman* in the interests of the Southern Confederacy, and to engage in piratical expeditions against Panama steamers and other commercial enterprises on the Pacific Ocean, which had been frustrated. The conspirators had escaped, and Meade turned up at Alder Gulch. I resented his insults somewhat, and for a moment there was evidence of dissent from his view. Dr. J. P. Maupin, who stood behind the counter, armed himself with a pick handle, but Mr. Creighton collared the braggadocio, and led him to the door, with warnings definite enough to be apprehended that he was expected to maintain peace.

I was the guest in Virginia City of Captain Nicholas Wall, who had erected a somewhat pretentious looking house at the rear of the store of John J. Roe and Co. which, with his nautical habit he had denominated "Texas," and which, for that time and place was an abode of no inconsiderable luxury. In the morning, upon awakening, I found our gentlemen outside the house guarding it on my account, of whom Mr. Michael Tovey and Conrad Weary were two, and guards remained with me and around my apartments until I left for Bannack.

At ten o'clock the next morning the meeting assembled again at Nevada for the disposition of the cases against George Hillerman and John Frank, but the strenuous controversy was over, the main criminal had been disposed of. Hillerman was an old weak, foolish man, doubtless without moral perception or cognizance of the crimes that were of daily occurrence and it was thought that, on the plane on which justice was administered at that time, it was not well to hang him, and after consultation with many of the leading citizens it was determined he should be banished and upon my motion it was made the duty of any person finding him in the settlements after New Year's to shoot him on sight. The lawyers reappeared with their passions somewhat allayed and their strenuousness perceptibly weakened, Messrs. Smith and Davis assuming the role of leading counsel for Hillerman. Hillerman desired to make a statement, and the privilege was granted him. He said nothing with reference to events in the country, but expressed a desire to be permitted to remain. He said he had no method of travel, and did not know how to go or where to go, to which a profane wit in the crowd responded by recommending to him a hot place beyond the confines of this world. The crowd, however, would not permit his presence, and he was ordered to go, with some arrangements made for his transportation, an opportunity of which he gladly availed himself, and his subsequent history is not known.

As to Long John, or John Frank, there was a universal belief that he had related truly such circumstances touching Tbolt's murder, and other murders and robberies in the country with frankness, and the animosity of the criminal classes towards him consequent thereto, strengthened the resolve to permit him to live and remain in the country till he should choose to depart, and he was discharged on Forefathers' Day, 1863, and the miners dispersed to their claims, the merchants to their stores, and other citizens to their several places of business.

Four days had been expended by at least fifteen hundred men out of deference to the forms of American institutions, and when the prosecutions were finished, and the community knew no more than it did when they were begun, a number of people began to inquire whether each tragedy required so much attention, and how much time would be left to pursue the ordinary vocations if this deference was to be continued, and speculations as to forming a vigilance committee grew in coherence and strength. We had our confidence strengthened by the splendid fidelity of the miners of Alder Gulch, and by their unshaken resolve that that which they achieved they would preserve, despite the robbers who had so long infested the country, and on the evening of the next day, I think it was, the nucleus of a Vigilance committee was formed, thereafter to grow to large proportions and to determine that in the heady struggle between order and crime, order should win the final mastery. But that is another story.

To Virginia City from Corinne, Utah, by Stage, 1873

When we reached Corinne, Utah, we had to take the stage. This seemed to me a real adventure. The stage coach was full, all seats taken. The favorite seat was by the driver "on the boot." By crowding, two people could sit outside with the driver. It is obvious that this outside seat was preferred except in the stormiest weather. The driver sat on the right side on top, his feet in the front boot. Why it was called a boot I don't know.

The driver was a distinguished individual. He wore fine calf-skin boots, into which, frequently, he tucked his pants. Usually he had on a fine woolen shirt, around his neck an elegant handkerchief or scarf. His head gear was a fine hat with a 2 or 2½-inch brim. He had doe-skin gloves, except in very cold weather when he put on silk gloves and red woolen mittens. As he drove four or six horses, he had to take his hands from the mittens occasionally to arrange the lines leading to the horses. In winter he used a short overcoat with a great leather band about his body, covering him from the armpits to his middle. Generally he was loquacious, and if so, he spoke in picturesque language, during which he indulged in weird similes to a greater or less extent. Besides, from the outside the traveler had many superb views. The inside of the stage coach usually had three seats. The back seat was sufficient for three people, who looked forward. The front seat was sufficient for three people also; these passengers sat with their backs to the driver, whom they couldn't see, and they looked backward. The middle seat was between the two, a little forward of the brake blocks. The passengers looked forward, their backs being supported by a leather band stretching from one side of the coach to the other. This leather was 10 to 12 inches wide. The middle seat was occupied when the passenger couldn't find another seat. This coach had a hind boot in which the trunks and other bags were carried. Usually the mail sacks were carried in the front boot. That most necessary appliance, the brake, was on the right. The driver operated it with his right foot. The vehicle was enclosed, roof and sides, with strong canvas. The openings for entrance and exit, one on either side, were protected by canvas "flaps." The bottom of the vehicle was wood planks, of course.

The journey from Corinne, Utah, to Virginia City, Montana, about 400 miles, was not a joyride. The passenger had to remain in his seat or lose it. No stopping over for a night's sleep. The next stage might be, probably would be, full. Passengers might alight for meals, and for urgent reasons. Otherwise the journey was continuous day and night. You may imagine the difficulty that confronted a mother with two small children.

We had not been out very long when we were joined by a platoon of cavalry, sent to protect us from the Indians who were on the warpath. The soldiers stayed with us a long time. These men were rigged out attractively, at least to a five year old boy. They had blue coats and breeches. There were brass buttons on the coats and some had chevrons on their arms. One had epaulets on his shoulders. All had yellow stripes down their breeches. They had pistols and guns, and one had a sword. All had spurs on their heels, and the horses made noises. I wanted to stand on the brake-blocks, holding onto the uprights, so I could see these soldiers all the time; but my mother objected. Just the same I would get out on the brake-block frequently, and she would make me get inside where I hated to be. She must have had plenty to do with taking care of the baby and looking after me.

In after years when the "Pioneers" were meeting in Virginia City (1899), Colonel Sanders was trying to amend the association's constitution; some were protesting against admitting "Pullman car pioneers." My mother said to Colonel Sanders, with whose endeavor she was sympathetic, that, while she didn't care to join the society, she wished some of those old fellows had to ride in a stage coach from Corinne with a baby not much over a year old and a five year old boy hanging outside a lurching coach, looking at soldiers keeping off hostile Indians.

When we got to Snake River there was something the matter with the ferry. We stood on the bank after nightfall, a grey stormy night, in the cold wind. I don't know for how long. It was tough. But all things end, and eventually the ferry took us across.

Somewhere in Montana my father met us with a buggy and conveyed us to Virginia City. What a relief it was to get in that buggy. The cavalry had left us long ago, and the stage was uncomfortable and monotonous.

Index